Lucifer's Lexicon

THE PORTABLE
L.A. ROLLINS

Lucifer's
Lexicon

with introduction by

MRDA

NINE-BANDED BOOKS +
UNDERWORLD AMUSEMENTS

ISBN 978-1-943687-17-6
REV: X.XX.MMXX

Published by
Nine-Banded Books
WWW.NINEBANDEDBOOKS.COM
and
Underworld Amusements
WWW.UNDERWORLDAMUSEMENTS.COM

Contents

Publisher's Preface

WHEN THE PARCEL I MAILED TO LOU was returned by the postal carrier, I assumed I had gotten the address wrong. I'm bad about that. So I set the thing aside and made a mental note to check it against the information I had on file, maybe give him a call to see if he'd moved. I let a couple of days pass and didn't think much of it. Then I happened to look more closely at the "undeliverable" postal stamp. That's when I noticed the checkbox was marked "deceased."

Could it have been a postal error? Doubtful, but I had to consider the possibility. I dreaded calling, so I contacted a longtime friend of Lou's by email. In short order, the bad news was confirmed. "I'm afraid," began the response that landed in my inbox hours after my inquiry, "that rumors of Lou's death have not been exaggerated at all."

Well, fuck.

•

In the years prior to his annihilation, Lou saw that my post office box was perpetually stuffed. On my weekly mail runs, I would unlock the little copper-plated door to find another batch of hand-addressed, multi-stamped business envelopes bulging with news clippings as well as Lou's own satirical poetry, letters, occasional essays, and—the burden of it—a seemingly endless supply of new or slightly revised material for a long-planned update of his best-known book, *Lucifer's Lexicon*. Everything he sent was written in longhand, scrawled with nary a spelling error

on hastily ripped spiral notebook pages.

When the mail stopped coming, I should have suspected something. Perhaps it did cross my mind. It's possible I was simply relieved. There was already so much to go through, as I had mentioned to him during our last phone conversation. Life gets busy. I suppose it wouldn't have mattered.

I still have the lot of Lou's correspondence compiled in a giant three-ring binder. A teeming, taunting transcription nightmare (see facing page).

The last mailing with a legible postmark was dated April 16, 2015. Lou's body was discovered in his apartment on May 6. Call it from there.

I don't know the cause of death. Supposedly, the coroner was investigating and would share a report with next of kin. That's long done by now, if it ever happened at all. It could have been any number of undiagnosed afflictions. Cancer. Heart failure. Maybe a fatal slip and fall. I don't suspect suicide (or ISIS assassins), not that it matters. Lou was, I think, 66. By all accounts, he was a ruined alcoholic—a devotee of what one of his friends described as "the cheapest, most godawful rotgut whisky imaginable." He was a hermit. He didn't tend to his health. He wasn't online. By reliable accounts, he had no social network. He had lost touch with his family.

"Abjection" is the word that comes to mind,

the word a biographer might prefer. I don't know. People live and people die.

Here is a *Lexicon* entry that Lou sent a couple of months before he bit the dust:

Death, *n.* A life going off after having gone on.

I do remember the last time I spoke with Lou over the phone. He was going on about Jesse Walker's book *The United States of Paranoia*. He liked it. He knew the history. He told me, not for the first time, that I should read something by James Branch Cabell. I made a note. He pointed out a couple of typos in a book I had published. I made another note. I encouraged him, not for the first time, to get a fucking Internet connection. He said the world had passed him by.

A few days later, Lou left me a drunken voicemail in the middle of the night. He was belting out the chorus to "Eddie's Teddy" from *The Rocky Horror Picture Show*. Key of Dr. Scott. Dead on, actually. It made me laugh. I never called him back.

Anecdotes are cheap. There was unfinished business. I suppose there always is.

•

Louis Andrew Rollins, better known to his small but devoted readership as "L.A. Rollins," was probably the least sentimental person I have ever known. When we were putting together an earlier collection of his writings—*The Myth of Natural Rights and Other Essays*—he sent me an obsessively comprehensive list of acknowledgments to close the book, but when he discovered that one of the people on his rollcall had died (I believe it was Samuel Konkin), Lou was emphatic that the name be removed before the book went to press. There was no point, he insisted, in thanking the dead.

I guess I'm not that far gone. Selfishly, and perhaps without justification,[1] I want to acknowledge Lou's time on this whirling rock. I want to thank his ghost for a few precious laughs and for the shape of thoughts, now mostly forgotten, that he once inspired or ignited. More

1   "Just a fixation," per *Lucifer's Lexicon*.

importantly, I want to share this with the living.

And I figure that's good enough reason to publish the man's extant writings—to attend to the "unfinished business" that I had more or less abandoned after the event of Lou's death. "Curation" is a trendy term these days. It comes up a lot in shop talk about the virtues of independent publishing. As far as I can tell, it just means "check this out." That's what Mike Hoy was saying when Loompanics released books by L.A. Rollins back in the 1980s, and that's what we're saying now.

I said "we," didn't I? That's because it probably wouldn't have happened were it not for Kevin Slaughter of Underworld Amusements, my co-publisher in this endeavor. In correspondence and conversation, Kevin was insistent that these texts needed to be reprinted. Whether we approached it as an exercise in libertarian archeology or for whatever resonance Lou's work might retain in counterpoint to the prevailing culture of trigger warnings and safe spaces or... just for kicks, it didn't matter. It was a thing, Kevin said, that needed doing. And I absolutely agree.

It was also Kevin's smart idea to go with a series of "portable" volumes rather than a stand-alone anthology. This approach has the advantage of showcasing the various facets of Lou's self-styled contrarianism—his Biercean wit, his incisive satire, his critical engagement with libertarian and Objectivist arguments, and his controversial dalliance with dissident history. Kevin knew it would go down easier in bite-size pieces. Kevin has good instincts—good *curatorial* instincts, one might say—in such matters. You can tell him I said so.

As you already know if you're reading this, we decided to kick things off with *Lucifer's Lexicon*. I'll have a few words about this edition shortly. First, a bit of background is in order.

L.A. Rollins received his B.A. degree in philosophy from California State College at Los Angeles in 1970 (which happens to be the year I was born). In the '70s, he edited and published a sporadic fringe-libertarian news-letter called *Invictus: A Journal of Individualist*

JUNE 1973

NO. 28

85cents

EGOISM:

Re-examined by Robert LeFevre

Defended by George H. Smith

ALSO:

free market garbage collection
(part one of a ten part series)

Thought (good luck finding a copy). As a free-lance writer, he contributed to a number of publications, including some respectable magazines like *Playboy*, *Reason*, and *Grump* as well as some not-so-respectable marginal rags like Samuel Konkin's *New Libertarian*, Bob Banner's *Critique*, and, more controversially, *The Journal of Historical Review.*[2]

So, he did that stuff. But I think it's a safe bet that L.A. Rollins will be best remembered as the author of two books, both of which were

2   Yes, I understand that Lou's straightforward—and actually highly critical—engagement with Holocaust revisionism proved to be "a bridge too far" for some otherwise amused readers. To me, it just made him more interesting. It's one thing to indulge in idle talk about slaying sacred cows; it's quite another to wield the bolt gun. Lou didn't think twice about this shit. And as for the Prophet Muhammad, *piss be upon him*.

originally published by Loompanics Unlimited (where Lou worked as a copyeditor) in the 1980s.

The first of these, which would probably be better described as a tract or monograph, was *The Myth of Natural Rights*. Still notorious in certain circles, *The Myth* was a sharply honed attack on the moral and political concept of "natural law," especially targeting such rebranded iterations of the concept that figured in the writings of libertarian luminaries like Tibor Machan, Ayn Rand, and Murray Rothbard. It created quite a stir when it was first released, as will be evidenced in the appendices to the new edition that we'll be publishing next.

Rollins' second book, *Lucifer's Lexicon*, took up the project of Ambrose Bierce's *The Devil's*

LUCIFER'S
LEXICON

BY L.A. ROLLINS

Dictionary, albeit in a less universal key. It was in *Lucifer's Lexicon* that Lou memorably defined the "Libertarian Movement" as "A herd of individualists stampeding toward freedom." That's the one people seem to remember, but there were others that tended to stick. I won't bother reciting my favorites since they're all collected in the pages that follow.

If you're of a certain age and of a certain intellectual temper, there's a good chance you'll recall your first brush with L.A. Rollins. You may remember him as a subcultural gadfly who stared down once-entrenched libertarian dogmas, or you may remember him as a scoundrel who strayed from the liberty-loving reservation to play footsie with historical outlaws. That's all wicked good fun, but it's more likely that the *Lexicon* is the thing that seared your synapses way back when.

After all, it was Lou's tongue-in-cheek stature as an "illustrious lexicographer" that, for a time, got him published in a diverse range of marginal and mainstream venues. The puns weren't always ready for prime time (neither were Bierce's, kids), but it's easy to forgive the occasional groaner when you ratchet back the lens to see the bigger game in play. You begin to see how Lou deployed nimble wordplay (and casual erudition) to skewer sacred spooks of every conceivable pedigree, often in "definitions" that branched into lengthy polemical essays.

In other words, the *Lexicon* is key. It's where to start, by curatorial decree. It provides the best introduction not only to Lou's undeniable nous as an underground satirist but to his more earnest endeavors as an equal-opportunity iconoclast. The version presented in the pages that follow includes the entirety of what might be called the "canonical" Loompanics edition along with scads of additional material culled from other sources and, of course, from the reams of correspondence that Lou supplied until his demise.

We considered date-indexing the sources, but that would have been difficult and probably distracting. In the end, we decided it would be better to just let the gears grind from time to time; therefore, dated references to Cold War intrigue and Reaganomics read alongside more contemporary jokes and commentary targeting, *inter alia*, ISIS shenanigans and neoconservative nostrums. It might make for a bumpy ride, but you can handle it. Suffice it to say, you may consider this the definitive edition. Unless we decide to do another one. I'm sure we left some good stuff on the cutting-room floor.

If you were there for the early rounds, consider this your chance to revisit that hazy terrain, whether out of nostalgia or to see what still jogs. There's plenty of new material to justify the price of admission in any case. Maybe some of the puns flew over your head the first time around? That was certainly the case for me.

And if you weren't ringside for the main event back then, this is your chance to discover the splenetic splendor that was and remains L.A. Rollins, *sui generis*. Be prepared to squint a bit— even the recent past is a foreign country—and be prepared to laugh.

As Lou was fond of saying, *make the most of it*.

CHIP SMITH
November 2018

Introduction

My familiarity with the works of L.A. Rollins goes back to 2006, a year anticipated in my boyhood as a time of flying cars, space exploration, meal pills, and transforming robots. The dream of a shining science-fiction future failed to materialize, but at least I had a freshly installed broadband connection, linking me to a myriad of fascinating websites and worldviews, to make up for it. As far as consolation prizes go, things could have been a *lot* worse.

My newly acquired upgrade from dial-up coincided with a nascent interest in the amoral strain of egoism, sparked a year earlier by my first reading of Max Stirner's *The Ego and Its Own* and sustained by my then-recent discovery of Harry Browne's more practical guide to living a super *einzige* life, *How I Found Freedom in an Unfree World*. Thus inspired, I trawled through every obscure site and shop that hinted at a sniff of similar fare until, through some byzantine sequence of events now long forgotten, I ended up getting my hands on a copy of *The Myth of Natural Rights*, my iconoclastic introduction to the world of L.A. Rollins. I'd read good things of it but nothing to prepare me for what lay in store.

To set the scene further, I'd spent the first half of the 2000s caught in the Randian wringer, leaving me more than familiar with the ins and outs of "natural rights" and "objective morality," and my reading of Stirner had yet to fully erase the residue. That promptly changed with the arrival of *Myth*, a lithe, black slip of a book put out by esteemed maverick publisher Loompanics Unlimited in the decade of my flying-car-fuelled fantasies, the '80s. Within a few pages, it became clear that, despite having credentials as a writer and publisher in the libertarian milieu, Rollins was the stark antithesis of a Randian or Rothbardian deontologist. "In my view," he declares in the tone-setting opening chapter, "natural law and natural rights are human *inventions* (not *discoveries*) intended to further the interests of the inventors." It only got more savage and scathing from there, with shearing talk of the gullible "two-legged sheep" enthralled to the nonexistent "bunk" of objective morality. By the end of the book, Rollins had put the sacred cows of many a libertarian luminary to the skewer, revealing the supposedly godless figureheads of the milieu to be yet more of the "pious people" Stirner had denounced a century earlier.

Though I would re-read *The Myth of Natural Rights*, and hunt down many of the works that Rollins cited therein, it would be a couple of years before I'd make my first encounter with the original edition of *Lucifer's Lexicon*. I managed to find it on the Stateside Amazon site, and about a fortnight later, it arrived in its full infernal glory. Thicker than *Myth*, and riffing off the similarly structured *Devil's Dictionary* by Ambrose Bierce, the Tabasco-toned tome contained wads of wordplay and witticisms aimed at making the reader laugh and think, sometimes in unison. Though not as relentlessly savage as his dissipation of the natural rights phantasm, the *Lexicon* had a sly impishness about it that kept me thoroughly amused. Sure, not every entry proved to be comedy gold, or to my taste, but the hits far outweighed the misses. I dare you to not crack at least a smile upon reading these exemplary gems:

Blowjob, *n.* A nice job if you can get it.

Deflower, *v.* To boldly go where no man has gone before.

Preacher, *n.* One who devotes his lips to the service of God.

Zionist, *n.* A bigot who wants the Jews to go back where they came from.

Around the time I procured the original *Lexicon*, Nine-Banded Books, helmed by one Chip Smith—an obscure publisher specializing in "recreational thoughtcrime for restive shut-ins"—put out an aesthetically enhanced, extended edition of *Myth* that featured an abridged chapter of Rollins' devilish definitions as part of the package—a sure buy! As well as many of the earlier entries, the carefully curated segment contained a few newer additions, such as the following:

Briton, *n.* One who keeps a stiff upper lip, especially during rigor mortis, after dying in a bombing.

Isolationist, *n.* A selfish bastard who stubbornly doesn't want to be bothered with slaughtering foreigners.

Neoconservative, *n.* A great American patriot whose only regret is that you have but one life to give for Israel.

Not to mention one of my enduring favorites:

Fountainhead, *n.* The very best kind of head, the kind that Ayn Rand used to give to Nathaniel Branden.

Now, more than a decade after that fateful purchase, I'm scribing and revising an intro for a new edition of the lightbearin' lexicon, a joint publication of Nine-Banded Books and Underworld Amusements (the latter helmed by another friend of mine, one Kevin I. Slaughter). Time marches on, even without flying cars (which are still more credible than all that "natural rights" bollocks!).

Sadly, L.A. Rollins is no longer with us, having passed away rather abruptly in the summer of 2015. This latest edition of *Lucifer's Lexicon* thus serves as the culmination of a project that was never really finished. We'll take what we can get, particularly with parting shots of this calibre:

Church, *n.* A place where Christians prepare for Heaven by enduring boredom. A place where but for the grace of Satan go I.

Inbred, *adj.* Having ancestors who were incestors.

Mariachi Music, *n.* A type of music so unpleasant that millions of Mexicans flee across the US border to escape it.

Pedophile, *n.* One who believes children should be obscene and not heard.

Make no mistake: If you enjoy acerbic aphorisms, impious insights, pernicious puns, and scorching satire (not to mention a good fucking laugh), this diabolical dictionary has all the devilry that you desire—and then some!

MRDA
November 2018
(Revised September 2020)

Lucifer's Lexicon

Abacus, *n.* A digital computer.

Abdicate, *v.* To quit one's job as a monarch in order to avoid being fired—or fired upon.

Abednego, *n.* One of three Jews, the others being Shadrach and Meshach, who were thrown alive into the fiery furnace on Nebuchadnezzar's orders and who survived, unlike the Jews more recently thrown alive into the fiery furnace on Hitler's orders. They don't make Jews like Shadrach, Meshach, and Abednego any more.

Abolitionist, *n.* One who advocated the abolition of slavery, presuming to know better than the God of the Bible, who did not abolish it.

Abomination, *n.* An action that puts God's

nose righteously out of joint, such as men having sex with men or anyone eating shrimp.

Abortion, *n.* The termination of a pregnancy with extreme prejudice. A preemptive strike against a potential terrorist.

Absolute, *adj.* Obsolete.

Abstract Expressionism, *n.* A bastard child of MoMA and Dada.

Abstraction, *n.* Obstruction.

Academia, *n.* Acanemia. The land of the acanemics, who live in Ivy-covered ivory towers.

Academic Freedom, *n.* Freedom to be academic.

Acapulco Gold, *n.* The possible basis for a commodity-money system that could be called the Acapulco Gold standard.

Acid, *n.* LSD. According to P.G. Stafford and B.H. Golightly, in *LSD: The Problem-Solving Psychedelic*, "a Hassidic rabbi after using a psychedelic danced in ecstasy with his tallith, declaring that his 'experience was truly religious, but wasn't "quite Jewish enough."'" Presumably, therefore, he did not become an Acidic rabbi.

Acidhead, *n.* One who trips the light fantastic and sings the body electric. (Of course, *bad* acid may turn an acidhead into a Ken Kwesey.)

Adam, *n.* The first name of the first man. His full name was "Adam Fool."

Addictive, *adj.* Having an inelastic demand curve.

Administer, *v.* To inflict, as a medicine, a sacrament, justice, or a government.

> With any government we are accursed
> And what is best administered is worst
> — Alexander Antipope

Admirer, *n.* One who sees himself in the mirror of another person.

Advertiser, *n.* A genius who trades in capitalist propaganda. For example, an advertiser has inscribed the following text on a plastic bag containing O-KE-DOKE Cheese-Flavored Popcorn: "Whenever somebody pops the question, 'What's the world's most fun snack?,' up pops the answer: O-KE-DOKE Popcorn!"

Advertising, *n.* The propaganda of commerce.

Affirmative Action, *n.* The white man's new burden. A system of handicapping used in the contemporary American rat race.

Afghanistan, *n.* Formerly, the Russian bear–trap. Now, the American eagle–trap.

Africa, *n.* The Darky Continent.

Afrocentrism, *n.* Clio (and Cleopatra) in blackface. Negro Cleopatriotism. A little black lie.

Agnostic, *n.* A God-fearing atheist.

Agriculture, *n.* The cultivation of legislators to raise subsidies. Pillage in the name of tillage.

Ahimsa, *n.* A Hindu and Buddhist doctrine of refraining from harming any living being—except yourself.

Ahmadinejad, Mahmoud, *n.* The new Hitler, according to the same old lying warmongers.

AIDS, *n.* The Gay Reaper. God's punishment for queers, junkies, and Haitians, all of whom have undoubtedly aroused His wrath. One of Mother Nature's meanest ways of being a wet blanket.

Air Superiority, *n.* The mother of moral superiority.

Akashic Record, The, *n.* An arcane archive consulted by theosophists, anthroposophists, and other sophists in order to write their revisionist histories of the world and the universe.

Albino, *n.* A whiter shade of paleface.

Alcoholic, *n.* One who searches for a message in every bottle. The message reads, "The world isn't as shitty as it seems."

Allah, *n.* One of a number of gods, each of whom is the only god.

Allahu Akbar!, *intj.* Strictly translated, this proclamation means "God is great, and I'll kill you if you don't agree, you infidel dog! Hell, I'll kill anyone I can get my hands on once I get going!"

Ambition, *n.* A desire to make something of oneself, such as a nuisance, a spectacle, or a fool.

Ambulance Chaser, *n.* A shyster who isn't shy.

Amen, *intj.* Right on, bro! Tell it like it am.

Amenable, *adj.* Willing to say "Amen."

America, *n.* A land where anything is possible, where any boy can grow up to be president. A pitiless, helpful giant. The Great Santa. The land of decree and the home of the slave. Columbia, the Purloined Gem of the Ocean. The greatest country on Earth. In fact, it's the greatest country on any planet, in any solar system, in any galaxy, in any universe, in any dimension! USA! USA! USA!

American, *n.* A sheep whose fleece is red, white, and blue.

American Cheese, *n.* Exceptional cheese. The greatest cheese that has existed in the history of the world.

American Exceptionalism, *n.* Brobdingnagian braggadocio. American deceptionalism.

American Interests, *n.* 1. Corporate interests. 2. Israeli interests.

Americanist, *n.* One who knows that America is the freest country on Earth but has no idea which is the second freest. One who loves the Liberty Bell—and resembles it as well.

American Nazi, *n.* One who goosesteps to a different drummer.

American Power, *n.* An exception to Lord

Acton's dictum that power tends to corrupt and absolute power corrupts absolutely. Why is it an exception? Don't ask me. Ask the exponents of the doctrine of American exceptionalism; I'm sure they'll have an exceptionally excellent answer.

American Way, The, *n.* My way. Norman Lear's way.

America the Beautiful, *n.* A land infested by ugly Americans.

Amicus Curiae, *n.* A friend of the court—and, therefore, an enemy of the people.

Amoralist, *n.* One from whose eyes the scales of justice have fallen. A Lysander Knifer.

Amotivational Syndrome, *n.* The psychological disorder that leads marijuana smokers to feel that nothing is worth doing except smoking marijuana. It is this lexicographer's guess that the late "Vietnam syndrome" was simply a specific aspect of a more general amotivational syndrome.

Amulet, *n.* Something worn to provide protection from harm, such as a four-leaf clover, a rabbit's foot, a St. Christopher medal, or Kevlar body armor.

Anarchist, *n.* One who advocates the separation of existence and state. A Thoreau-going Jeffersonian democrat. A master-baiter. A slave of anarchism. One who prefers Emma Goldman to Golda Meir. One who does his duty to Durruti. One who realizes that the ship of state is a pirate ship. One who is *on* his rocker—Rudolf Rocker, that is.

Anarchy, *n.* A Hobbes-goblin. The ideal state of affairs in which there is no state to stop anarchist sectarians from taking direct action—killing each other off. The absence of government and the resulting state of utter chaos as hordes of former government employees run amok, rioting, looting, raping, and pillaging. Anarchy is a very naughty state of affairs—or, perhaps I should say, a naughty no-state of affairs. Consider the following horrible example drawn from Michael Brooks' *Free Radicals* (The Overlook Press, NY, NY, 2011, page 206):

> At the outbreak of the Spanish Civil War, the people of Barcelona took control of the city's street railways. Anarchy ensued: not anarchy as disorder or chaos, but anarchy as removal of the ruling classes. The worker's union took over the railways and dismissed the directors, who had been paid eighteen times what the average railway worker earned. With the directors gone, the wages of the lowest earners went up 50 percent. What's more, the unions were able to radically improve the efficiency of the system. Fares were reduced, and certain members of the population—schoolchildren, invalid wounded soldiers, and those who had suffered injuries at work—were allowed to travel for free. What started on the railways soon made its way to the ports, the utility companies, the clothing industries—even the hairdressers. Catalonia became an anarchist state. In many ways, it still is.

Anchorperson, *n.* A talking figurehead. A dishonest Brokaw of misinformation.

Ancient, *adj.* Existing or occurring in the distant past, such as before the 1960s.

Anglo, *n.* A polite synonym for "aringo."

Animal Liberationist, *n.* One who seeks to liberate animals from mistreatment by humans but not from mistreatment by other animals. One who defends the equality of dogs with the dogma of equality. One who opposes the oppression of opossums. One who champions the rights of chimpanzees. One who battles on behalf of cattle. One who fights for the rights of rats. One who proves that egalitarianism is for the birds. A villain who victimizes vegetables.

Animal Rights, *n., pl.* The rights of animals, such as the right of lions to be fed Christians.

Animal Shelter, *n.* A death camp for dogs and cats. In 1978, Guy Hodges, a director of the Humane Society, gave the following information to the Associated Press: More than 7.5 million dogs end up in animal shelters each year. Only one in 13 of those dogs will ever be adopted or returned to their owners. Except for a small percentage used in research and therapy, most of the other 6.9 million will be destroyed with an injection of barbiturates, the most humane method, causing death in a matter of seconds; some are gassed with carbon monoxide; others are destroyed in decompression chambers, where they die from lack of air. Most animal shelters cremate the dogs on the premises, others are taken to landfills, and a small number are used by industry, such as for making soap. Some furriers buy dog skins. All in all, it's a veritable *holocaust* of hounds.

Anoint, *v.* To pour oil upon a messiah or some other slippery character.

Anthem, *n.* A sacred hymn. A song of patriotism or devotion. Here, for example, is Ambrose Bierce's "A Rational Anthem":

> My country, 'tis of thee,
> Sweet land of felony,
> Of thee I sing—
> Land where my fathers fried
> Young witches and applied
> Whips to the Quaker's hide
> And made him spring.
> My knavish country, thee,
> Land where the thief is free,
> Thy laws I love;
> I love thy thieving bills
> That tap the people's tills;
> I love thy mob whose will's
> All laws above.
> Let Federal employees
> And rings rob all they please,
> The whole year long.
> Let office-holders make
> Their piles and judges rake
> Our coin. For Jesus' sake,
> Let's all go wrong!

Also, a song of allegiance, such as the following:

> Atlantis, 'tis of thee,
> Sweet land of fantasy,
> Of thee I sing,
> Land of Blavatsky's pride,
> Where black magicians died.
> Round every oceanside
> Let myth be king.

Anti-Arabism, *n.* The other anti-Semitism. Fortunately for many American bigots, this prejudice is perfectly kosher.

Anti-Defamation League, *n.* The Pro-Doublethink League. The Zionist Thought Police. An organization working for B'nai B'rith control. A group of bloodhounds smelling after "anti-Semitism." As George Orwell once wrote (in a letter to a friend), "Some people go around smelling after anti-Semitism all the time. There is more rubbish written about this subject than any other I know of." If the Anti-Defamation League says that war in Lebanon is peace in Galilee, that censorship is free speech, that Holocaust studies is strength, or that two plus two equals six million, then it must be true. Winston Smith loves B'nai B'rith.

Anti-Gentilism, *n.* Talmudslinging.

Anti-Imperialism, *n.* The last refuge of an imperialist.

Anti-Racism, *n.* A prejudice more acceptable than others.

Anti-Racist, *n.* One who is prejudiced against the prejudiced and intolerant of the intolerant; one who hates the haters and discriminates against the discriminators.

Anti-Semite, *n.* 1. One who hates Jews. 2. One who is hated by Jews.

Anti-Zionism, *n.* A code word for "anti-Semitism," just as "Zionism" is a code word for "anti-gentilism."

Apartheid, *n.* A policy requiring blacks and whites to hate each other separately but equally.

Apathy, *n.* The sin of being indifferent toward the indifferent, of not caring whether one is ruled by Tweedlecrat or Tweedlepublican.

Apostate, *n.* A state for an ex-apostle.

Apostle, *n.* A fisher of men who uses the worm of immortality as bait.

Apostolic Succession, *n.* The regular and uninterrupted transmission of spiritual authority from the apostles of Jesus to the bishops of the Anglican, Eastern Orthodox, Roman Catholic, and various other churches.

Appeaser, *n.* A pejorative term used by warmongers for one who wants to keep the peace.

Appendix, *n.* An otherwise useless organ placed in the human body by a benevolent Creator in order to provide work for surgeons.

Apple, *n.* A fruit which is reputedly a doctor-repellent.

Aqua Vitae, *n.* The water of life. Also known as whiskey.

Arab, *n.* A second-rate Semite.

Arab–Israeli Conflict, *n.* The War of the Noses.

Arcadia, *n.* A region characterized by simple pleasure and quiet surroundings, located northeast of Los Angeles, California.

Argument from Intimidation, _n._ In the words of Ayn Rand, who identified this informal fallacy, the argument from intimidation

> is not an argument, but a means of forestalling debate and extorting an opponent's agreement with one's undiscussed notions. It is a method of bypassing logic by means of psychological pressure .... the psychological pressure method consists of threatening to impeach an opponent's character by means of his argument, thus impeaching the argument without debate. The essential characteristic of the Argument from Intimidation is its appeal to moral self-doubt and its reliance on the fear, guilt or ignorance of the victim. It is used in the form of an ultimatum demanding that the victim renounce a given idea without discussion, under threat of being considered morally unworthy. The pattern is always: 'Only those who are evil (dishonest, heartless, insensitive, ignorant, etc.) can hold such an idea....

For one real-life example of the argument from intimidation, see David Hamlin's _The Nazi/Skokie Conflict: A Civil Liberties Battle_ (1980). Hamlin, one of the ACLU lawyers who defended American Nazi Frank Collin's civil right to march in Skokie, Illinois, says that when the first news accounts of the controversy reached the public, all hell broke loose. Among the many angry phone calls received at the ACLU's Chicago office, one was from a man who identified himself as a lawyer and "suggested that only the son of parents who had served as guards in Hitler's camps could take the position I argued."

For another example of the argument from intimidation, see a letter appearing in _The Nation_

(2 May 1981) by Michael Blankfort of Los Angeles (perhaps the same Michael Blankfort who was a playwright, novelist, and screen-writer, who, in an interview shortly before his death in July 1982, said that a visit he made in 1948 resulted in "the onset of a devotion to Israel that is without parallel in my life"). He wrote, "Anyone who claims the Holocaust never happened is insane. Why shouldn't a university fire a crazy teacher who might harm his students with his criminal delusions?" In other words, only the insane can hold the idea that the Holocaust never happened. Coincidentally, Thomas Szasz, in *The Manufacture of Madness* (1970), mentioned a doctor of the Sorbonne who wrote in 1609 that the Witches' Sabbat was an objective fact, disbelieved only by those of unsound mind. The parallel is obvious—and ominous.

Armadillo, *n.* A poor man's pig. Some people angry with Herbert Hoover called the armadillo a Hoover hog during the Great Depression…or, rather, the First Great Depression.

Armageddon Theology, *n.* Banging the Bible and beating the war drums. The Christian belief that the future looks bright, indeed, brighter than a thousand suns. This is the way the world ends, not with a whimper but with a Bible bang. Blessed are the warmongers, for they shall be blown to Kingdom Come.

Armed Robbery, *n.* A form of practical alchemy, by means of which lead can be turned into gold.

Arms Control, *n.* People control. I'm sure the folks at the John Birch Society will agree that when weapons of mass destruction are outlawed, only outlaws will have weapons of mass destruction.

Ass, *n.* One who cannot tell himself from a hole in the ground.

Assad, Hafez, *n.* The leader of the Syrian Blood Ba'ath Party.

Associate, *n.* A glorified wage slave.

Assure, *v.* To evoke uncertainty.

Astral Plane, *n.* A mumbo-jumbo jet.

Atheist, *n.* One who is as omniscient as the deity whose existence he denies. One who does not believe in God but is still holier than thou. A Biblebanger-basher. A theist.

Atlas Shrugged, *n.* A science-fiction novel set in the past.

Atomic Age, *n.* The age of atomic bombs and other miracles performed by our saviors, the scientists.

Atrocity, *n.* A cruel or brutal act taken not out of military necessity but military luxury.

Au Jus, *n.* Aw, juice.

Auschwitz, *n.* A World War II Nazi concentration camp subsequently turned into a Commie tourist trap.

Austerity, *n.* Having to tighten one's belt, perhaps around one's neck prior to hanging oneself.

Austrian Economics, *n.* An explanation of "human action" that fails to explain the actions of humans.

Austrian Economist, *n.* One who is more interested in Friedrich Hayek's mind than Salma Hayek's body.

Auto-da-fé, *n.* A ceremony in which heretics are burned to provide them with a sneak peek of what they'll be in for in Hell.

Avant Garde, *n.* Shock troops of the new. The lemmings in the lead.

Awake, *adj.* Asleep.

Axis of Evil, *n.* Excess of bullshit.

Ayatollah Khomeini, The, ***n.*** The Shi'ite Shah.

Bachelor, *n.* A man in a state of nature in which life is solitary, poor, nasty, brutish, and short.

Bahaism, *n.* A religion that disagrees with all other religions in teaching the agreement of all religions.

Bald Eagle, *n.* A bird of prey—and, therefore, a symbol of the United States.

Baloney, *n.* A very popular type of food for thought.

Bank Robbery, *n.* 1. A robbery of a bank. 2. A robbery by a bank or banks, such as the $700 billion bank bailout of 2008.

Banquet, *n.* 1. A sumptuous feast. 2. A pre-sumptuous frozen dinner.

Barbarian, *n.* One who does not speak Greek. This lexicographer is a barbarian. He does not speak Greek. It's all Greek to him.

Based on a True Story, *phr.* Not a true story.

Basket Case, *n.* A soldier who has said a farewell to arms—and legs.

Bathory, Elizabeth, *n.* A victim of patriarchy.

Bay of Pigs, *n.* Pigs at bay.

Beast, The, *n.* The Secret Service code name for Barack Obama's new presidential limousine. What's with the Secret Service? Are they trying to drive Bible-prophecy nuts even nuttier than they already are by suggesting that Obama *is* the Antichrist, as some prophecy nuts have already been speculating? (Note: CNN and some other sources have given "The Beast" as the code name for the limo, but I now see other sources giving contradictory information, such as that the code name is "The Stagecoach.")

Beatnik, *n.* One who prefers the ecstasy of the Negro night to the humdrum of the Caucasian daylight.

Beauty, *n.* Truth, according to one of Keats' beautiful lies. A heresy, according to many modern artists.

Bedbug, *n.* A consolation to one who would otherwise be sleeping alone.

Begin, Menachem, *n.* An Ashkenazi war criminal still at large. One of the murderers among us whom Simon Wiesenthal is not hunting.

Behaviorist, *n.* A psychologist who wants to make people behave. A Pavlovian dogmatist, salivating as the bell tolls for freedom. For example, B.F. Skinner, author of *Buchenwalden Two* and *Beneath Freedom and Dignity*.

Beheading, *n.* A penal measure involving the removal of an offender's head from his body so that the former might no longer exert an evil influence upon the latter.

> A hashish peddler was judged by King Faisal.
> The king said, "Beheading's a just reprisal."
> Said convict to monarch 'ere scimitar did swing,
> "I give undying thanks. 'Tis a fate fit for a king!"
> —Kahil Al-bran

Being, *n.* A philosopher's spook, otherwise known as nothingness.

Belief, *n.* A fig leaf used to cover up one's ignorance.

Believer, *n.* An opinion addict.

Bermuda Triangle, *n.* A section of the western Atlantic Ocean, off the southeast coast of the United States, where truth has mysteriously vanished into thin air.

Berserker, *n.* A Norse warrior who fought with frenzied fury, invulnerable to fire and iron, unlike his decadent descendants.

Bestiality, *n.* Doing it doggy-style—with doggies. Petophilia. Of course, anyone who discriminates against nonhuman animals in selecting sex partners is simply a human-speciesist pig.

Bible, *n.* A literary work attributed to God, though, in fact, it was wholly ghostwritten. One of the many words of God. Among the other words of God are the Koran, the Book of Mormon, and *Lucifer's Lexicon*.

Bible Belt, *n.* The belt that holds up the pants of Southern Baptists, except for those of Jim Bakker, Jimmy Swaggart, etc.

Biden, Joseph, *n.* Joe AIPAC, politically a more important person than Joe Sixpack.

Bierce, Ambrose, *n.* A writer who was wittier than Whittier.

Big Bang, The, *n.* A creation myth favored by scientists.

Big Lie, *n.* Grand perjury.

According to Roland Baker in *Liar's Manual* (1983),

> Vladimir Ilyich Lenin, the leader of the Russian Revolution of 1917, was a very astute man. He is credited with the famous observation that the masses, meaning the people, will believe a big lie more readily than a small one.
> No doubt the masses had been lied to hugely long before Lenin's time. However, Lenin does deserve credit for making the observation on his own, stating it succinctly and with some flair, and for popularizing the idea.

Was Roland Baker telling a "big lie" when he

wrote this? The reason I ask is that it was Adolf Hitler, not Vladimir Lenin, who is credited with popularizing the idea of the "big lie." In *Mein Kampf*, Hitler wrote,

> It required the whole bottomless falsehood of the Jews and their Marxist fighting organization to lay the blame for the collapse on that very man who alone, with superhuman energy and will power, tried to prevent the catastrophe he foresaw and save the nation from its time of deepest humiliation and disgrace. By branding Ludendorff as guilty for the loss of the World War they took the weapon of moral right from the one dangerous accuser who could have risen against the traitors to the fatherland. In this they proceeded on the sound principle that the magnitude of a lie always contains a certain factor of credibility, since the great masses of the people in the very bottom of their hearts tend to be corrupted rather than consciously and purposely evil, and that, therefore, in view of the primitive simplicity of their minds they more easily fall a victim to a big lie than to a little one, since they themselves lie in little things, but would be ashamed of lies that were too big. Such a falsehood will never enter their heads and they will not be able to believe in the possibility of such monstrous effrontery and infamous misrepresentation in others; yes, even when enlightened on the subject, they will long doubt and waver, and continue to accept at least one of these causes as true. Therefore, something of even the most insolent lie will always remain and stick—a fact which all the great lie-virtuosi and lying-clubs in this world know only too well and also make the most treacherous use of. The foremost connoisseurs of this truth regarding the possibilities in the use of falsehood and slander have always been the Jews; for after all, their whole existence is based on one single great lie, to wit, that they are a religious community while actually they are a race—and what a race! One of

the greatest minds of humanity [Schopenhauer]
has nailed them forever as such in an eternally
correct phrase of fundamental truth: he called
them 'the great masters of the lie.' And anyone
who does not recognize this or does not want to
believe it will never in this world be able to help
the truth to victory.

That is what Hitler wrote about the "big lie."
Thus, when Azriel Eisenberg, in *Witness to the
Holocaust* (1981), wrote that "Hitler glorified
the 'big lie,'" he too was telling a "big lie." And
when, according to Michael Hoffman II in *The
Great Holocaust Trial* (1985), German-Canadian
Holocaust revisionist Ernst Zündel "brought
part of *Mein Kampf* into court and quoted
verbatim Hitler's words which actually state
that this 'Big Lie' technique is a method of the
Zionist establishment," he was also telling a
"big lie."

According to Roland Baker,

it is known that Richard Nixon, when he was
a young man, once won a debate by making up
a quotation. He had the audacity to do it. Was
there anybody in the audience who could have
known that there was no such quotation?

A fascinating aspect of this adventure is that,
knowingly or not, Nixon utilized a lying method
that is very difficult to expose....

In Nixon's case, reference was made to an
invented quotation. Inventing a quotation was
a big lie: He simply stated without proof in the
presence of many something he wished were
true. This was done without any preparation
or skillful blending of facts and fiction, and
the statement was about a material fact—the
existence of a given quotation. But the fact that
the quotation was invented was very difficult

to prove. It was not a known fact that such a quotation did not exist

To catch or cast suspicion on Nixon, you would have to furnish what is known as 'negative proof.' This means that you would have had to prove that something did not happen. This is extremely difficult, and sometimes impossible, to do....

Richard Nixon is not the only one who has used this variation of the "big lie" technique. In an interview with reporter Timothy Carlson of the *Los Angeles Herald Examiner* (2 February 1981), Holocaust survivor Mel Mermelstein used an invented quotation to "prove" that the Nazis, on Adolf Hitler's orders, had mass-murdered Jews in gas chambers. Carlson quoted Mermelstein, referring to the writings of Holocaust revisionists:

It's the same vein today, 36 years later, [as when] Goebbels reassured Hitler he ought not to worry about the consequences of the Final Solution of the 'Jewish Question,' .... Goebbels said to Hitler that because of the way the Germans were doing it—luring Jews into gas chambers disguised as shower rooms—*what* the Germans were doing was so inconceivable, it will be unbelievable. The civilized world will simply dismiss it as a hoax, he said.

Of course, for the reasons given by Roland Baker, I cannot conclusively prove that Goebbels never said this to Hitler. But if you doubt that this is an invented quotation, then simply ask Mel Mermelstein [defunct address and phone numbers redacted—Ed.] to provide some evidence that Goebbels did in fact say it. You might find the experience extremely educational.

Bilingual, *n.* Capable of uttering doubletalk in two languages.

Bilocation, *n.* Being in two places at once, a piddling little miracle compared to trilocation, quadrilocation, quintilocation, etc. According to Robert Siblerud in *Keepers of the Secrets*, "Legend had [Sufi] master Rumi concurrently attending seventeen different parties, and writing a poem at each."

Bin Laden, Osama, *n.* A freedom fighter, according to Ronald Reagan. A terrorist, according to George W. Bush. As the saying goes, one Republican's freedom fighter is another Republican's terrorist.

Biological Warfare, *n.* The kind of cultural exchange program once preferred by Cold Warriors.

Bircher, *n.* One who loves America no matter how much he comes to hate it. One who Birches about what's happening in the world.

Bisexual, *n.* A switch hitter, able to strike out either way.

Black Atlantis, *n.* The title of this lexicographer's book proving that Atlantis was the first civilization and that it was a black civilization.

Black Death, ***n.*** The means by which God wiped out much of the population of Europe in the 14th century, thereby providentially creating a shortage of labor that enabled workers to demand and get better pay.

Black-Eyed Peas, *n., pl.* Black-eyed beans.

Black Lung, *n.* Beautiful lung.

Black Market, *n.* The under-the-counter-economy.

Black Middle Class, *n.* The jigabourgeoisie.

Black Muslims, *n., pl.* Allah God's chillun.

Black Sheep, *n.* One who has a b-a-a-a-d attitude.

Blair, Tony, *n.* George W. Bush's poodle. Not a French poodle but a "freedom poodle."

Blame America Firster, *n.* The term used by Blame America Neverers to refer to anyone who ever criticizes America's rulers, who, of course, are above criticism. Yes, sitting up there on top of that huge pile of money, our rulers are *way* above criticism.

Blarney, *n.* The Irish word for baloney. A pot o' gold at the end of a rainbow painted by a leprechaun artist.

Blasphemer, *n.* One who pisses on Christ and pisses off Christians.

Blog, *n.* Blague.

Blood, *n.* A liquid that is thicker than water but not as thick as oil.

Blowjob, *n.* A nice job if you can get it.

Blues, *n.* A form of music performed by blind, illiterate blacks and enjoyed by deaf, college-educated whites.

Boeing, *n.* The sound made by airplane parts bouncing off the ground.

Bohemian Grove, *n.* The place where the rich and powerful gather to worship Moloch, an owl god, according to Alex Jones, who apparently worships some sort of bull god.

Bolshevik, *n.* A homicidal humanitarian.

Bombing, *n.* Trenchard warfare.

Bonaparte, Napoleon, *n.* A madman, obviously—he thought he was Napoleon!

B-1, *n.* A vitamin essential to the health of the military-industrial complex.

Book, *n.* A box of thoughts. A set of written, printed, or blank sheets bound together. What about eBooks? To hell with eBooks, computards! As for real books, here are some outstanding titles: *A Sale of Two Titties; Mascaramouche; Writers of the Purple Prose; Craven New World; God's Glossary; Candide Yams; Jurgen Off; The Picture of Dorian Gay; The Tragedy of Birth; Thus Spake Crazy Freddie; Ant Farm; The Teenage Titfuckers of Titan; Piano Player; A Clockwork Lemon; Tit Can't Happen Here; The Ghorman-Ghastly Trilogy; The Planet of the Grapes; Antony Flew Over the Cuckoo's Nest; The Myth of Mental Health; Do Adenoids Dream of Electric Tonsils?; Warpaths of Glory; Airport Noise Complaint; Slaughterhouse 459; Pnincompoop; Invitation to a Decapitation; Kilgore Trout Fishing in America; The Treasure of the Sierra Maestra; Conan the Librarian; Catcher 23 in the Rye; My Ammonia; Ship of Educated Fools; The Voyage of the Damned*

Jews; The Cunt is a Lonely Hunter; We, The Living Dead; The Fountainbleu; Lord Jack; The Man Who Was Thursday Afternoon; The Chronicles of Hernia; The Fnord of the Rings; Harry Potter and the Holy Grail; Da Godfadda; The Gang That Could Only Shoot Gays; The Fnord of the Flies; An Economic Interpretation of Yo Mamma's Pussy; Lavender Boy; Breakfast at Tiffany Thayer's; Sex and the Single Hermaphrodite; The Feminist Mistake; The Female Unicorn; The Last Eunuch; Watergate Down; A Farewell to Arms and Legs and Even Cocks; The Sun Also Sets; For Whom the Tell Bowls; Fickleberry Hun; The Prince and Karl Popper; A Connecticut Honky in Shaka Zulu's Convent; Don't Cry, The Beloved Country; The Armeniazation of Emily; The Man with the Gray Flannel Mouth; The Virtue of Shellfishness; Johnny Got His Irgun; Capitalism: The Ideal Unknown; The Manischewitz Candidate; The Burnt Umber Heresy; From Prussia, with Hate; For Your Thighs Only; Russian to Judgment; On the Trial of the Assassins; Where Beagles Dare; The Goons of Navarone; The Steel Heel; Lady Loverly's Chatter; The Topic of Cancer; Nun Island; The Man Who Ate His Own Liver; Vex Us, Hex Us, Texas; Captain Fellatio; Madame Ovary; Turpentine and Dandeloon Wine; Something Wicker This Way Comes; The Tattooed Dude; Finkelstein; The Apprenticeship of Fuddy-Duddy Kravitz; What Makes Sammy Run Amok?; Dr. Chicago; The Goulash Archipelago; Winnegan's Fake; God and Yo Mamma at Yale; The Conscience of a Conservative Advocate of Mass Murder and Total War; The Monkey Wenching Gang; Babbleit; Insanity Fair; A Critique of Pure Bullshit; The Girl Who Giggles; The Halfback of Notre Dame; In Defense of Wolfmen; Cashmere Christianity; The

Mars Bonfire of the Vanity; Steppenfetchit; Damien; Mencken It; Don't Do It; Revolution for the Halibut; Censor This Book; Winning Through Incineration; Third Reichian Therapy; We Have Ways of Getting You in Touch with Your Feelings (Especially Pain); Real Men Don't Eat Stacy Keach; The Oy of Sex; Spinsterhood Is Powerful; Profiles in Chutzpah; Up From Optimism; Inveigling We Will Go; The Pursuit of Assholiness; My God Is Bigger Than Your God; Ben Her: The Story of a Transexual in the Time of Jesus Christ; Dress for Suck Sex; God Damn You, Mr. Roosevelt; The Wizard of Szasz; The Toxic Kool-Aid Hydrocyanic Acid Test; No Existentialism; The Scarlet Pimp; The Strange Case of Dr. Jeckyll and Mr. Heckyll; Looking Ass-Backward; I Land; The Doors of Deception; Bullshit Abounding; The Diarrhea of Anne Frank; Revisionism for the Hell of It; The Jokes of the Twentieth Century; Inquest of Truth and Justice; The Lighter Side of Genocide; The Man Who Invented 'Chronocide'; Inferium; War Makes a Racket; Wall Street and Antony Sutton; The Naked W. Cleon Skousen; Trilateral Thinking; You Can Trust Fred Schwartz (to Be Fred Schwartz); Conservatism, Rheumatism, and Lawrence Welk; The Protocols of the Learned Elders of Nylon; What Color Is Your Paranoia?; Who Killed Oswald?; The Second Hitler; The Illuminerds; Cosmic Nigger, or The Final Secret of Ishmael Reed; The State Against Whites; Toots; The Cocaine Mutiny; The Faking of a Counterculture; The Gruening of America; The Ecstasy of Politics; For a New Dawn of a New Day of a New Beginning of a New Birth of a New Liberty for a New America; Capitalism and Friedman; Libertarianism as a Revolt Against Nature; Post-Anarchy Scarcitism; The Smith of Natural Rights; My Ego and My Own;

How I Found Freedom in a Six-foot-by-Twelve-foot Prison Cell; This Bread is Mined; Offending the Unoffendable; Never Trust a Naked Book Writer; Fromm Escapes Freedom; The Pseudo-Philosophy of Tibor R. Machan; Certainty Without Knowledge; The Rand–Brandon Dichotomy; Who Is Ayn Rand, and Why Is She Saying Those Terrible Things About Me?; Ayn's Kampf; Love and Sex in the Bedroom of Ayn Rand; Objectivism: The Perversion of Objectivity; The Virtue of Viciousness: A New Concept of Sadism; Cannibalism: The Unknown Ideal; For the Jew Intellectual; Philosophy: Who the Fuck Needs It?; The Acidhead; Atlas Fugged; I Was a Teenage Randroid; Lust in Space; and *The Zero-Gravity Sex Manual.*

Book-Burning, *n.* Censorship in the 451st degree. Chances are you've heard that the Nazis burned books, as indeed they did on 10 May 1933. But have you heard that the office warehouse of the Institute for Historical Review, an American publisher of revisionist history books, was largely destroyed by arson in the early morning hours of the 4th of July 1984? Some of the books in the IHR's inventory were literally burned. Thus do some fanatical "anti-Nazis" ape the tactics of Nazi beasts. Could it be that those who never forget the past are condemned to repeat it? But never mind, dear reader. Don't worry your pretty little head about it. Just stick it back in the sand, and keep telling yourself, over and over, "It can't happen here. It can't happen here. It can't happen here…"

Book Club, *n.* A weapon used to bludgeon readers into submission.

Born Again, *adj.* Fooled again.

Born Again Christian, *n.* One who has been brainwashed in the blood of the Lamb.

Bowel Movement, *n.* The only kind of movement there is.

Brainwashington, D.C., *n.* The capital of the United States.

Breast, *n.* A feminine appurtenance provided by a thoughtful Creator for the nourishment and pacification of babies of all ages.

Breatharian, *n.* One who claims that man can live by breath alone. *Breatharians of the world, unite! You have nothing to lose but your food chains!*

British, *adj.* Pertaining to Mediocre Britain, its people, customs, etc.

British Israelite, *n.* An Anglo-Saxon who thinks he sees the Lost Tribes of Israel perching in the upper branches of his family tree. In 1946, Dr. Thomas Walsh, a Catholic historian, summed up the doctrine of the British-Israel World Federation in the following words:

> This cult is apparently Masonic in origin. It professes to derive its tenets from prophecies inscribed on the Great Pyramid. Briefly, these revelations are supposed to indicate that the Anglo-Saxons comprise two of the lost tribes of Israel, one in England, the other in the United States; that these, and not the ostensible Jews, were the Chosen People of God; that they have been appointed by Destiny to rule the whole world; that this will be accomplished in 1947 by

the union of Britain and America in one common citizenship, and that in 1953 a world ruler will take command not only of these favored nations, but of all lesser breed without the law. This world leader will be the true Christ, come to establish his kingdom on Earth. He will be a descendant of King David. And by a strange coincidence many of these sectaries claim that the present King of England and his brother, the Duke of Windsor, are descended from the royal ancestor of Our Lord and Savior Jesus Christ.

Of course, as we know, it all came to pass precisely as prophesied. Hallelujah!

Briton, *n.* One who keeps a stiff upper lip, especially during rigor mortis, after dying in a bombing.

Broadcasting, *v.* Casting swill before millions of swine.

Broadcast Journalism, *n.* Salanted news.

Broadway Musical, *n.* An extreme example of the Theater of Cruelty.

BS, *n.* An abbreviation for "Belief System."

Buchenwald, *n.* A notorious Nazi concentration camp and a much less well-known Commie concentration camp.

Buck, *n.* The *bête noire* of the white racist.

Buddy, *n.* A total stranger from whom one wishes to mooch something. Synonyms include "pal," "brother," "bro," and "amigo."

Budget Cut, *n.* Formerly, a decrease in government spending. Now, a decrease in the rate of increase in government spending.

Bullhorn, *n.* A device used to amplify bullshit.

Bullshit, *n.* A fertilizer essential to the growth of civilizations.

Bully, *adj.* Excellent. A usage favored by Theodore Roosevelt (who was not himself bully, though he was a bully).

Bureaucracy, *n.* A perpetual inertia machine.

Bush, George W., *n.* A very likeable man who is loathed and abominated by billions of people, not because of anything he has ever done, mind you, but only because of who he is, a very likeable man.

Bushwa, *n.* Anything ever said by a Bush, or a bush, especially a burning one.

Café au lait, *n*. Coffee with milk, not to be confused with "café olé," which is coffee with bull's blood.

Caffeine, *n*. The poor man's cocaine.

Cakewalk, *n*. The neoconservative euphemism for a quagmire.

Call Girl, *n*. A woman who lets your fingers do her walking.

Callous, *n*. What you can develop by doing callousthenics.

Calvary, *n*. The skull without the bones.

Campaign, *n*. In US politics, a race in which a horse's hind end almost always wins.

Campaigning, *v.* In American politics, meeting the press and pressing the meat.

Canada, *n.* An expurgated paperback edition of the United States.

I have in my possession several pages of the list of titles of books banned by Canadian Customs from importation into that country. Here are the (real) titles of some of those banned books: *Abused by Arab Sadists; All America Must Know THE TERROR That Is Upon Us; All in the Family; Anal Slut; Antichrist; Auschwitz Slave; Behind Communism; Between Mom's Hot Thighs; Big Brother Game; Bizarre Rubber Fantasy; Black Bitch; Bondage Babe; Britain's Blunder; Cellblock Beefcake; Come-Hungry Cruiser; Complete Guide to Lockpicking; Daughter's Doggie Ways; Deadlier Than the H-Bomb; Death Dealer's Manual; Dominant Transvestite; Family Sex Festival; Gangbanged Girl Scouts; Germany and Peace—A Soldier's Message; Gestapo Bondage Brothel; Gestapo Lust Slave; Gestapo Sex Crimes; Gestapo Sex Training; Gestapo Torture Camp; Gestapo Toy; Gestapo Training School; Get Even; Great Holocaust Trial; 120 Questions and Answers; House of Torment; How to Make Your Own Professional Lock Tools; I.D. For Sale; Incestuous Longings; International Jew; Japanese Torture Isle; Jewish-Run Concentration Camps in the Soviet Union; Journal of Historical Review; Journey of Torture; Kinky Degradation; Leather Bound; Library of Political Secrets; Life of an American Jew in Racist, Marxist Israel; Madame Pain; Morgenthau Era Letters; My Nympho Aunt*

Joyce; Myth of Marxism; Naked Nuns: Their Strange Sexual Rituals; Nameless War; Nature's Eternal Religion; Nazi Butcher; Nazi Gassings: A Myth?; Nazi Sadists; Nazi Sex Captives; Nazi Sex Cult Bared; Nazi Torture Shack; New I.D. in America; None Dare Call it Conspiracy; Nun in Bondage; One Day in the Life of Ivan Denisovich; Onward Christian Soldiers; Prisoners of the Iranian Sadists; The Proclamation of London of the European Liberation Front; Raped by Arab Terrorists; Red Fog Over America; Rulers of Russia; Saigon Hell Hole; Secret Powers Behind Revolution; Secrets of the Ninja; Shackled for Rape; Slave Girls in Torment; Slave Orgy; Slaves of Auschwitz; Sluts of the SS; Spanking Daddies; Straight Look at the Third Reich; Three Bulls Meet the Rubbermaster; Truck Stop Sex Slave; Truth About the Protocols; Ultimate World Order; Underage Housewife; Up Yours!; Used by the Gestapo; Victim of the Gestapo; Viet Cong Torture Shack; Violent Stories of Lesbian Brutality; Voodoo Rape Orgy; Whips of Chinatown; and *Zionism Rules the World.*

In 1984, Arthur Butz's *The Hoax of The Twentieth Century* was placed on this banned books list at the behest of The League for Human Rights (heh, heh) of B'nai B'rith Canada, represented by Alan Shefman. Citing the Customs ban as legal justification, the RCMP subsequently seized copies of Butz's book from the library of the University of Calgary. The Mounties always get their banned book, right?

Cancer, *n.* Any dangerous and spreading evil. According to Susan Sontag in *Illness as Political*

Metaphor (1978),

> "To describe a phenomenon as a cancer is an incitement to violence. The use of cancer in political discourse encourages fatalism and `severe' measures—as well as strongly reinforcing the popular perception that the disease is necessarily fatal. The concept of disease is never innocent. But it could be argued that the cancer metaphors are in themselves implicitly genocidal. No specific political view seems to have a monopoly on this metaphor. If Hitler called the Jews the cancer of Europe, Trotsky called Stalinism the cancer of Marxism, and in China in the last year the Gang of Four have become, among other things, `the cancer of China.' John Dean called Watergate `the cancer on the presidency.'"

And for that matter, writing in *Partisan Review* in 1967, Susan Sontag said,

> "The white race *is* the cancer of human history; it is the white race and it alone—its ideologies and inventions—which eradicates autonomous civilizations wherever it spreads, which has upset the ecological balance of the plant, which now threatens the very existence of life itself."

Candid, *adj.* Honest and open; sincere; frank. This is the root word of "candidacy," which means "Honesty and openness; sincerity; frankness."

Candidate, *n.* A box of soap not quite 99 and 44/100ths percent pure. One who lusts in his heart for political power.

Cannibal, *n.* One who believes it's not what you eat but *who* you eat that matters. One who eats split-brain soup. One who eschews curds and whey but might eat Kurds and whey. One who eats refried beaners. One for whom fingers are finger food. One who might enjoy frogs' legs, as well as other body parts of Frenchmen. One who eats crackers. One who thinks there's always room for Jello—Jello Biafra. One who thinks vegetables go well with vegetarians. One who eats bacon—such as Roger Bacon or Francis Bacon. (Incidentally, among revisionist literary historians, Francis Bacon has been a popular candidate for the role of "true author of the plays attributed to William Shakespeare." But take it from me, kiddies—and I am omniscient and infallible—the plays attributed to William Shakespeare were actually written by six chimpanzees who banged on typewriters for a million years.)

Capital, *n.* A seat of deceit.

Capitalism, *n.* Moneytheism. The ideal politico-economic system, in which one can sell one's soul to the highest bidder.

Capital Letter, *n.* The form of a letter used to start a sentence—or a movement (see "Bowel Movement").

Captive Nations, *n.* Nations.

Caribbean Basin, *n.* Another sink in which American money is drained.

Case Closed, *phr.* Mind closed.

Casual Sex, *n.* Sex that is easy come, easy go.

Catastrophism, *n.* The theory adhered to by fundamentalist Christian geologists that attributes the present geological structure of the Earth not to gradual changes but to catastrophic events such as the Noachian Flood and the first and foremost catastrophe, the Creation.

Catechism, *n.* Dogmatism.

Categorical Imperative, *n.* Kant implies "ought not."

Cathedra, *n.* The seat of authority, as in the dictum "*Ex cathedra nihil fit.*"

Catholic, *n.* A papist. Sometimes also a rapist.

Catholicism, *n.* Christian Phariseeism.

Catnip, *n.* An aromatic herb of the mint family of which some cats, including some two-legged ones, are fond. Some cats, however, prefer hemp.

Celebrant, *n.* The officiating priest at the Eucharist, who consecrates bread and wine, miraculously transforming them into his bread and butter.

Censor, *n.* One who puts offensive authors and artists in their place—in jail. Remember, no matter how overcrowded the jails may be, there's always room for Jello Biafra. One who seeks a monopoly on the opportunity to peruse pornography. One who enlightens the world by burning books. Paradoxically, however, burning books, as enlightening as it is, also has a chilling effect.

Censorship, *n.* Vee haff vays uff making you shut up.

Certainty, *n.* A state of mind consistent with ignorance.

Channeling, *v.* A New Age answer to television that is less entertaining than changing channels.

Charisma, *n.* A kind of magnetism that attracts lead.

Chauvinism, *n.* Egotistical collectivism.

Chemical Warfare, *n.* Better things for better killing—through chemistry.

Chicago, *n.* A city on the lake—and on the make.

Child Abductor, *n.* A whippersnapper-napper.

Chiweenie, *n.* A beaner-weiner.

Chosen People, The, *n.* The Jews, considered as God's pets: an idea produced by Jewishful thinking. The self-chosen people.

According to Dennis Prager and Joseph Telushkin in *Why the Jews?* (1983),

> Jewish chosenness has always meant that the Jews have believed themselves chosen by God to spread ethical monotheism to the world and to live as a moral "light unto the nations" "*Isaiah*, 49:6). *All other meanings imputed to Jewish chosenness are non-Jewish.*

> The Hebrew Bible, where the concept origi-
> nates in its entirety, neither states nor implies
> that chosenness means Jewish superiority or
> privilege....

But consider the following passage from the
King James Version of the Bible:

> The LORD shall establish thee an holy people
> unto himself, as he hath sworn unto thee, if thou
> shalt keep the commandments of the LORD thy
> God, and walk in his ways.
>
> And all people of the earth shall see that thou
> art called by the name of the LORD; and they
> shall be afraid of thee.
>
> And the LORD shall make thee plenteous in
> goods, in the fruit of thy body, and in the fruit of
> thy cattle, and in the fruit of thy ground, in the
> land which the LORD sware unto thy fathers to
> give thee.
>
> The LORD shall open unto thee his good trea-
> sure, the heaven to give the rain unto thy land
> in his season, and to bless all the work of thine
> hand: and thou shalt lend unto many nations,
> and thou shalt not borrow.
>
> And the LORD shall make thee the head, and
> not the tail; and thou shalt be above only, and
> thou shalt not be beneath; if that thou hearken
> unto the commandments of the LORD thy God,
> which I command thee this day, to observe and
> to do *them*...

Apparently, the "ethical monotheism" espoused
by Prager and Telushkin does not require them
to tell the truth. Or perhaps God simply made a
mistake in choosing Prager and Telushkin to be
a moral light unto the nations.

Christian, *n.* A fable-minded person. One who
uses a cross as a crutch. One who shoots up
with a steeple. One who fixes with a crucifix.
One who has a lamb on his back. A pope fiend.

A Cathaholic. One who has a monk on his back. One who expects to be saved by the Calvary.

Christian Anarchist, *n.* One who loves his enemy, the state.

Christian Conservative, *n.* One who is proud to be an Ugly American, even though pride is a sin. A blind guide who strains out a zygote but swallows a full-grown camel jockey.

Christianity, *n.* The bastard child of Judaism and paganism.

Christian Men's Movement, The, *n.* A movement involving Christian men who gather together out in their inner Wildmon. For more information, see Donald Woldmon's book, *Iron John, the Baptist*.

Christian Science, *n.* Strictly speaking, a contradiction in terms. The science of the lambs. A belief system for which all illnesses and injuries are psychosomatic. That bullet that's lodged in your brain? Actually, it's all in your mind.

Christian Zionist, *n.* A liar twice over: Christian Zionists lie because they are Christians, and they lie because they are Zionists.

Church, *n.* A place where Christians prepare for Heaven by enduring boredom. A place where but for the grace of Satan go I.

Churchgoer, *n.* One who goes regularly to church, for one reason or another.

Churchill, Winston, *n.* A belligerent drunk. The greatest hero of the twentieth century and a homicidal maniac. (Recommended reading: *Human Smoke* by Nicholson Baker.)

Churl, *n.* An uncouth boor. In Anglo-Saxon England, the word meant "a freeman," and its transformation to the present meaning was perhaps the most beneficial consequence of the Norman Conquest.

CIA, *n.* The Conspiratorial Intervention Agency.

Circe, *n.* A sorceress who turned men into swine. Not much of a trick since men are already swine.

Circumcision, *n.* A form of cosmetic surgery vulgarly known as a "dick job."

City, *n.* Hell and heaven on Earth.

Civics, *n.* The study of a citizen's privileges, rights, and duties. For example, it is a citizen's privilege to pay taxes, it is his right to be represented in the body that levies taxes, and it is his duty to evade taxes.

Civil Forfeiture, *n.* Theft by cops.

Civil Libertarian, *n.* A phony First Amendment fundamentalist who pretends to defend our sacred freedom to complain about our slavery.

Civilization, *n.* Savagery enhanced by gadgetry.

Civilized, *adj.* Tamed.

Clairvoyeurism, *n.* Using one's psychic powers to be a Peeping Tom.

Clash of Civilizations, The, *n.* The clash of barbarisms.

Climate Change, *n.* A warmed-over apocalypse for secular doomsayers.

Cloning, *n.* The xeroxing of living things.

Cluster Bomb, *n.* A big bomb containing a lot of cute little bomblets just the right size for maiming and killing cute little kids.

Coalition of the Willing, The, *n.* A folie à deux.

Cockroach, *n.* An uninvited guest in many urban residences. According to a news story I read some years ago, cockroaches are a good source of protein. If this is true, then I would like to know:Who *really* needs food stamps?

Coffee, *n.* A popular drink, the psychoactive ingredient of which is caffeine. A beverage containing caffeine, a psychoactive and addictive substance. When a coffee drinker kicks the habit all at once, it is known as "going cold perky."

In 1902, T.D. Crowthers, M.D., published *Morphinism and Narcomanias from Other Drugs*, wherein he discussed coffee addiction. "In some extreme cases," he wrote, "delusional states of a grandiose character appear; rarely violent or destructive, but usually of a reckless, unthinking variety. Associated with these are suspicions of wrong and injustice from others; also extravagant credulity and skepticism." Speaking as a caffeine fiend myself, I agree with almost everything the doctor wrote, which only goes to show my extravagant credulity.

Cold Turkey, *n.* Pulling the drug out from under an addict.

Cold War, *n.* The Evil Empire versus the Good Empire. The Soviets were evil because they lied and killed to get what they wanted. We lie and kill because we are good.

Collective Leadership, *n.* In the Soviet Union, the cult of impersonality. Socialism with no face at all.

Collective Security, *n.* A diplomatic arrangement for the maintenance of world peace through world war.

Commissar, *n.* A Commie czar.

Commitment, *n.* In international relations, a statesman's solemn pledge that somebody else will do something.

Committee of 300, The, *n.* The most secret society in the world, according to Dr. John Coleman, the most full-of-shit conspiracy writer in the world. (Okay, maybe Coleman isn't the *most* full-of-shit conspiracy writer. Maybe Lyndon LaRouche is more full of shit. Or David Icke. Or William Guy Carr. Or F. Tupper Saussy. Or.... In any case, Coleman is definitely one of the most full-of-shit conspiracy writers in the world.)

Common Good, *n.* The good for those who use the expression "the common good."

Common Knowledge, *n.* Something generally known among the ignorant.

Common Sense, *n.* The faculty that enables one to see the obvious truth, such as that the Earth is the center of the universe around which all else revolves.

Communism, *n.* A Marxian chimera. Utopia in the sky-blue future.

In *The German Ideology*, Marxandengels wrote,

> in communist society, where nobody has one exclusive sphere of activity but each can become accomplished in any branch he wishes, society regulates the general production and thus makes it possible for me to be one thing today and another tomorrow, to hunt in the morning, fish in the afternoon, rear cattle in the evening, criticise after dinner, just as I have a mind, without ever becoming hunter, fisherman, shepherd or critic.

Poor Marxandengels! How he must have suffered, living in a capitalist society, in which he had to spend his time criticizing without ever having the chance to hunt or fish or rear cattle.

Communist China, *n.* A hybrid offspring of the Red Menace and the Yellow Peril—in short, the Orange Danger.

Communist Party, *n.* In the Soviet Union, the vanguard of the bureaucrats.

Compassion, *n.* A candidate's pity for the suffering or distress of eligible voters, along with the desire to help, if elected.

Competition, *n.* The rivalry between lobbyists striving for the same political patronage. A means by which capitalists collaborate to advance their common interests.

Compulsory Drug Testing, *n.* Urination of sheep.

Conceptual Artist, *n.* One who conceives of himself as an artist. Also known as a "con artist."

Concerned Citizen, *n.* One who believes it is better to give a shit than to take a shit.

Confession, *n.* 1. An admission of wrongdoing, often obtained by wrongdoing. 2. An act of confessing one's sins to a priest. I've heard rumors that in some particularly tough neighborhoods, the priests use rubber hoses to extract confessions.

Confidence, *n.* A feeling of trust in a confidence man.

Conformist, *n.* A bleatnik. One who marches to the beat of the same old humdrummer. One who, when in Xanadu, does as the Xanaduans do.

Congress, *n.* A nest of vultures, simultaneously feathering and fouling their habitation. The opposite of progress.

Connoisseur, *n.* One who insists on only the very best port, even in a storm.

Conscience, *n.* Nonscience.

Conscientious Objector, *n.* A sacred coward.

Conscript, *n.* One forced to fight for freedom.

Conservative, *n.* A class warrior on behalf of the rich who pretends that class warfare is very naughty in order to disarm the non-rich classes. One who favors limited government and total war. One who is against exercise because Jane Fonda is for it. As Franklin Roosevelt said, "A conservative is a man with two perfectly good legs who, however, has never learned to walk." Of course, Roosevelt forgot to add that a liberal is a cripple who wants to force somebody else to pay for his wheelchair.

Considerate, *adj.* Thoughtful of others and what they can do for you.

Consistency, *n.* A straight and narrow path leading to fanaticism. Consistency was Ayn Rand's primary criterion for correctness. Rand failed to note that consistency is also consistent with being wrong about everything.

Conspiracy, *n.* The secret side of politics; the underside of the rock. Piracy on the secret sea.

Conspiracy Theorist, *n.* One who is devoted to giving conspiracy theory a bad name. One who says the pope is not Catholic. One who knows all the secrets of all the secret societies. But how? Obviously, he must be a member!

Conspiracy Theory, *n.* A theory about a

conspiracy that you are not supposed to believe. A theory about a conspiracy that you *are* supposed to believe is not called a "conspiracy theory" but simply a "conspiracy" (or some other synonym, such as "plot"). A way for non-Marxists to wage class warfare against the rich and powerful.

A theory about a conspiracy, such as Alvin Rosenfeld's theory about an Arab Muslim conspiracy to destroy Israel, which he expounded in his 1977 book, *The Plot to Destroy Israel*. As Rosenfeld so cogently noted, the Arab Muslim countries of the Middle East would never dream of fighting against each other, so the only possible reason for their acquisition of weapons was to use them to destroy Israel, which, of course, is exactly what they did.

Conspiratologist, *n.* One who has wheels within wheels in his head. One who is only a pawn in his own mind game. One who is lost in the labyrinth behind Leviathan. A paranoid Peter Beter. One who knows the pope is not Catholic. One who asks, "Who killed Kennedy?" But I say, Ask not "Who killed Kennedy?" but, rather, "Who did Kennedy kill?"

Conspiratologists are dedicated to *the truth*. That is why William Guy Carr, in *Pawns in the Game*, wrote,

> John Quincy Adams had organized the New England Masonic Lodges. In 1800 he decided to oppose Jefferson for the presidency. He wrote three letters to Colonel Wm. L. Stone exposing how Jefferson was using Masonic lodges for

subversive purposes. The information contained in the letters is credited with winning Adams the election. The Letters are in Rittenburg Square Library, in Philadelphia.

And that is also why William Guy Carr's disciple, Des Griffin, in *Fourth Reich of the Rich*, wrote,

In 1796, John Adams, who had been instrumental in organizing Masonic Lodges in New England, decided to oppose Thomas Jefferson in his bid for the presidency. He made a major issue of the fact that Jefferson—who had been minister to France, 1785–1789, and was frankly sympathetic to the Illuminist-fomented Reign of Terror—was using Masonic lodges for subversive purposes. John Quincy Adams wrote three letters to Colonel William L. Stone giving details of the charges. The information contained in these letters is credited with winning John Adams (his father) the election. The existence of these letters was first brought to the public's attention by Commander William Guy Carr in his book, *Pawns in the Game*. Until recently they were in the Rittenburg Square Library in Philadelphia. They have now mysterioulsy vanished.

Of course, as all good conspiratologists know, evidence which has "mysteriously vanished" is the best evidence of all—since it can never be conclusively disproven.

Constitution, The, *n.* The health of the state. A holy writ for the American twit. A constitution that was unconstitutionally substituted for the original US constitution, the Articles of Confederation.

Consumerism, *n.* The pursuit of happiness through the purchase of crappiness.

Contactee, *n.* A stratospheric status-seeker who drops the names of extraterrestrials. In his 1955 book, *Inside the Space Ships*, George Adamski reported at great length his conversations with Firkon of Mars, Ramu of Saturn, and Orthon of Venus, all of which proved that George Adamski was a Very Important Earthling. According to David Michael Jacobs, in *The UFO Controversy in America*,

> "George Hunt Williamson, one of the alleged witnesses to Adamski's first contact, claimed he could communicate with men from Mars by using a ham radio set and a Ouija board.... Dana Howard went to Venus, married a Venusian, and raised a family—all while she was napping on her living room couch"

Controlled Substance, *n.* A substance that is not controlled, although the government might be trying to control it.

Controversy, *n.* A clash of symbols. A battle in which bullshit substitutes for bullets.

Copernicus, *n.* The man who replaced the delusion of geocentrism with the delusion of heliocentrism.

Corporate Capitalism, *n.* Collectivist capitalism.

Corporation, *n.* A union of capitalists who disapprove of unions of employees. In the words of Ambrose Bierce, "An ingenious device for obtaining individual profit without individual responsibility."

Cosa Nostra, *n.* Literally translated, this term means "Our Thing." Thus, the Cosa Nostra is simply a group of Italian American counterculturists doing their thing.

Cosmology, *n.* The study of the universe as a hole.

Coulter, Ann, *n.* America's favorite female-impersonator. Coulter does an especially good job of simulating stereotypical female illogicality, as, for example, when "she" writes that the fact that Jesus is still hated is the best argument there is for the truth of Christianity. This makes as much sense as saying that the fact that Muhammad (piss be upon him) is still hated is the best argument for the truth of Islam.

Count Saint Germain, *n.* Author of the first 2,000 Year Old Man routine. His version was more original than Mel Brooks' but not as funny. "Ascended Master of the 76th Degree" and former "Chohan of the 7th Ray." Pretty impressive credentials, huh? By some accounts, Count Saint Germain was the "Hidden Architect and Creator of the United States of America." But then, by some other accounts, Lorenzo Ricci, the 18th "Superior General of the Society of Jesus," was the Hidden Architect and Creator of the United States of America. In this case, as in some others, we seem to have duelling conspiracy theories.

Court Historians, *n.* Historians who drool over those who rule.

Cover-Up, *n.* An attempt to hide something, such as evidence of a criminal conspiracy or the weak points of one's conspiracy theory.

Creationist, *n.* One who knows that humans are not animals, which is why humans don't eat, drink, defecate, urinate, or copulate.

Credibility, *n.* Ability to deceive.

Criminal Regime, *n.* Regime.

Critical Thinker, *n.* One who thinks critically about the things he thinks critically about and thinks gullibly about the things he thinks gullibly about.

Cross, The, *n.* A symbol of the crucifixion of Jesus Christ. Can also be used as a dildo.

Crusade, *n.* A jihad for Jesus.

Cryptocracy, The, *n.* A figment of the paranoid Christian-fanatic imagination of one Michael A. Hoffman II. Although Hoffman has used the term in *Secret Societies and Psychological Warfare* and other writings, he has never presented a detailed, coherent history of "the cryptocracy." He can't because it doesn't exist.

CSICOP, *n.* A skeptic tank.

Cuckold, *v.* To sympathetically put oneself in another man's place in order to experience his feelings.

Cui Bono? Latin for "Who can I blame?"

Cult, *n.* A religion that is disapproved of, especially if it is smaller and less powerful than
other religions. Past and present cults include
Jews for Jesus, Christians for Krishna, Quakers
for Quetzalcoatl, Zoroastrians for Zeus,
Sciencefictionology, the Dead Peoples Temple,
the Latter-Day Sinners, etc.

Culture Wars, *n., pl.* Dueling delusions.

Cynicism, *n.* The sin of doubting the sincerity
of hypocrites.

Dada, *n.* Nada. Thus spake Tzara-thustra.

Dairyman, *n.* One who milks the public, not with his own hands but with the state's arms.

Damnation, *n.* In theology, eternal punishment decreed by a cruel and unusual god.

Dangerous Drugs, *n., pl.* Drugs.

Darwinism, *n.* A dogma that did not evolve from a wolfma.

Deadwood, *n.* The raw material used to make school boards, Federal Reserve Boards, the planks of political platforms, government bureaus and cabinets, and presidential timber.

Death, *n.* A life going off after having gone on. An essential part of the American way of life. Something to live for.

Decadence, *n.* The idolization of idiosyncrasy. Sleeping with Satan on satin sheets. Sowing one's Wilde oats while going against the grain.

Declaration of Independence, *n.* An artifact of Revolutionary War propaganda. The United States' declaration of its independence from Great Britain. This lexicographer is awaiting, but not holding his breath while doing so, the United States' declaration of its independence from Israel.

Defend, *v.* To stick up for after sticking up.

Deflower, *v.* To boldly go where no man has gone before.

Deist, *n.* One who believes in a Creator who, following Creation, has behaved like a gentleman, minding his own fucking business.

Delirium Tremens, *n.* Elephantasmagoria.

Deluge, *n.* A worldwide flood by means of which God drowned all humans and animals on Earth except for the select few on Noah's Ark, proving that God is not a pro-lifer.

Demjanjuk Trial, *n.* A Jerusalem witch trial. A Shoah trial. Fuck 'em if they can't take Demjewjokes.

Democracy, *n.* Government of the sheep, by the shepherds, for the wolves.

Democrat, *n.* One who fights parsimony with sanctimony.

Democratic Party, *n.* The "good cop" to the Republican Party "bad cop." The party of war and treason. The Republican Party is the exact opposite, the party of treason and war.

Depraved, *adj.* In touch with one's inner sinner.

Depression, *n.* A cloud whose silver lining is most easily perceived by a psychotherapist— since it enables him to line his pocket with silver.

Deprogramming, *n.* Reprogramming. Brainwashing contra brainwashing.

Deranged, *adj.* No longer home on the range.

Devil, The, *n.* The Prince of the Kingdom of Evil. As Cotton Mather wrote in *A Discourse on the Wonders of the Invisible World* (1692),

> That there is a devil, is a thing doubted by none but such as are under the influences of the devil. For any to deny the being of a devil must be from an ignorance or profaneness, worse than diabolical.

Far be it for me, therefore, to deny the existence of the Devil. Rather, let me quote the following description of His Lowness given by Agnes Simpson, a confessed Scottish witch, in 1590:

> His body was hard lyk yrn, as they thoct that handled him; his face was terrible, his nose lyk the bek of an egle, gret bournyng eyn: his handis and legis were herry, with clawis vpon his handis and feit lyk the griffon.

Dictatorship, *n.* Government by force and fraud, as opposed to democracy, government by fraud and force.

Dignity, *n.* The stateliness and nobility of manner characteristic of a welfare mother.

Diplomacy, *n.* Duplicity.

Diplomat, *n.* A mat it is not polite to walk on, though it is sometimes done nonetheless.

Disaster, n. Good news for journalists—and for premillenial dipsensationalists.

Disciple, *n.* In the words of Robert Anton Wilson, "an asshole looking for a human being to attach itself to."

Discordian, *n.* An advocate of Eristocracy. A Fnordic supremacist. A Thornley in the side of authority. One who takes religion too Siriusly. A devotee of Confusionism. One who wears Emperor Norton's old clothes.

Discovery, *n.* The finding of something one was not looking for.

Discrete, *adj.* Sneaky in a classy way.

Dittohead, *n.* One who rushes to misjudgment.

Divine, *adj.* Of or pertaining to the vine, specifically the True Vine, the source of the True Wine, i.e., Dionysus.

Dixon, Jeane, *n.* The true mastermind behind the conspiracy to assassinate JFK.

Docudrama, *n.* History according to Hollywood, the Land of Make-Believe. Why is it that none of the critics who lambasted Abby Mann for the historical distortions in *The Atlanta Child Murders* has ever expressed the slightest doubt about the absolute accuracy of his Academy Award–winning earlier docudrama, *Judgment at Nuremberg*?

Dog, *n.* The satanic way to say "God."

Dogma, *n.* A bitch of a belief. A fixed idea that hasn't been fixed. Dogmas come in many breeds, including the Holy Ghost and the Holocaust.

Do-Gooder, *n.* An evildoer; a malefactor of melioration; a crusadist; one who has nothing better to do.

Dogwood, *n.* A tree whose bark is worse than its bite.

Do-Nothing, *adj.* Doing no harm.

Double Taxation, *n.* Taxing the income of investors or corporations twice. This is anathema to Republicans, who don't seem to mind the triple or quadruple or quintuple taxation of the income of employees.

Doubt, *n.* The philosophical device Descartes so cleverly used to prove everything he previously believed.

Downsizing, *v.* The destruction of jobs by job creators.

Draft, *n.* An ill wind from which many a young man has caught his death.

Draft Dodger, *n.* An impious miscreant who jumps out of the way of a juggernaut.

Dress Code, *n.* Don't suit yourself—suit us.

Drug Abuser, *n.* One who maligns drugs.

Drug Czar, *n.* A pharmacological pharoah. A despot-head.

Dualism, *n.* Duelism.

Dual Loyalist, *n.* Disloyalist. One who pledges allegiance to the Stars and Stripes out of one side of his mouth while pledging allegiance to the Star of David out of the other.

Dumpster Diving, *n.* Discardianism. For more information, see the book *Principia Discardia, or How I Found the Goodies and What I Did With Them After I Found Them.*

Dye, *n.* Matter used to color cloth. In *Women's Dress,* Tertullian (the Mr. Blackwell of the early Christian Church) denounced the use of dye:

> What value is given cloth by adulteration with false colors? God likes not that which He Himself did not produce. Had He not the power to order that sheep should be born with purple or sky-blue fleece? He had the power, but He had not wish; and what God did not wish certainly ought not to be produced artificially.

One wonders, however, what the implications of such an argument might be with respect to books not written by God—books such as Tertullian's *Women's Dress,* for example.

Economist, *n.* One who enjoys a comparative advantage with regard to producing bullshit.

Edit, *v.* To prepare for publication, sometimes by removing offensive material. If you think this book is offensive *now*, you should have seen it *before* it was edited.

Education, *n.* Propaganda of which one approves.

Effeminacy, *n.* The state or quality of having feminine traits to a degree not befitting a man. It is most commonly encountered in women.

Efficient, *adj.* In physics and engineering, giving a relatively large output per unit of input. In economics, "good for the rich."

Egalitarian, *n.* A morally superior person. A

person so blind, s/he will not see the difference between a hero and a zero, a champ and a chump, a winner and a wiener, or a king and a kong. One who believes inequity is iniquity. A member of the Not-See Party. One who is Philip Green with envy.

Egalityranny, *n.* A state of comprehensive, compulsory egalitarianism, in which it is illegal to discriminate against anyone or anything for any reason. Is this not where we are now headed?

Eggplant, *n.* A plant that is not an egg.

Ego, The, *n.* The spook that haunts the heads of Stirnerites.

Egoism, *n.* The only "ism" for me.

Egoist, *n.* A nation of one. A Max Monad. One who is made of Stirner stuff.

Eichmann Trial, *n.* Trial by Jewry. As Lenny Bruce said,

> Eichmann really figured, you know, 'The Jews—they'll give me a fair shake." Fair? Certainly. "Rabbi" means lawyer. He'll get the best trial in the world, Eichmann. Ha! They were shaving his legs while he was giving his appeal.

Einstein, Albert, *n.* A comedian whose stage name is "Albert Brooks."

Elitist, *n.* One who looks down his snotty, snobby nose at those he regards as inferior to himself, quite possibly correctly.

Enlightenment, *n.* 1. Thinking. 2. Not thinking.

Entertainment, *n.* Something that diverts or amuses, such as Fred Astaire dancing on Ginger Rogers, Gene Kelly romancing Donald O'Connor, Ed Asner being tortured by Argentinian anti-Semites, Vanessa Redgrave playing the dual role of a Palestinian terrorist who hijacks an airplane *and* an Auschwitz survivor who is one of the passengers, Al Pacino playing Cliff Gorman playing Dustin Hoffman playing Lenny Bruce, Jack Nicholson tit-fucking Ann-Margret, or a Mel Brooks comedy about the Holocaust—*Blazing Shtetls*. That's entertainment!

Epistemologist, *n.* A cat chasing its own tail.

Epistemology, *n.* The theory of knowledge, as distinguished from the knowledge of knowledge.

Equality, *n.* A quality that exists only in mathematics.

Eternal bliss, *n.* Eventual boredom.

Ethnocentrism, *n.* The opinion that one's group is the center of the universe, around which all else revolves, and that one's group is more important than any other. Ethnocentrism is one thing all groups have in common. Consider this passage from Edward Westermarck's *The Origin and Development of the Moral Ideas*:

According to Eskimo beliefs, the first man, though made by the Great Being, was a failure, and was consequently cast aside and called kob-lu-na, which means "white man"; but a second attempt of the Great Being resulted in the formation of a perfect man, and he was called in-nu, the name which the Eskimo give to themselves. Australian natives, on being asked to work, have often replied, "White fellow works, not black fellow; black fellow gentleman." When anything foolish is done, the Chippewas use an expression which means "as stupid as a white man." If a South Sea Islander sees a very awkward person, he says, "How stupid you are; perhaps you are an Englishman." Mr. Williams tells us of a Fijian who, having been to the United States, was ordered by his chiefs to say whether the country of the white man was better than Fiji, and in what respects. He had not, however, gone far in telling the truth, when one cried out, "He is a prating fellow"; another, "He is impudent"; and some said, "Kill him." The Koriaks are more argumentative; in order to prove that the accounts they hear of the advantages of other countries are so many lies, they say to the stranger, "If you could enjoy these advantages at home, what made you take so much trouble to come to us?" But the Koriaks, in their turn, are looked down upon by their neighbours, the Chukchi, who call the surrounding peoples old women, only fit to guard their flocks, and to be their attendants. The Ainu despise the Japanese just as much as the Japanese despise them, and are convinced of "the superiority of their own blood and descent over that of all other peoples in the world." Even the miserable Veddah of Ceylon has a very high opinion of himself, and regards his civilised neighbours with contempt. As is often the case with civilised men, savages attribute to their own people all kinds of virtue in perfection. The South American Mbayás, according to Azara, "*se croient la nation la plus noble du monde, la plus généreuse, la plus exacte à tenir sa parole avec loyauté, et la plus vaillante.*" The Eskimo of Norton Sound speak of themselves as *yuʹ-pɪˇk*, meaning fine or complete people, whereas an Indian is termed *iñ-kɪˇ-lɪˇk*, from a word which means "a louse egg." When a Greenlander saw a foreigner of gentle and modest manners, his usual remark was, "He is almost as well-bred as we," or, "He begins to be a man," that is, a Greenlander. The savage regards his people as the people, as the root of all others, and as occupying the middle of the earth. The Hottentots love to call themselves "the men of men." The Indians of the Ungava district, Hudson Bay, give themselves the name *nenenot*, that is, true or ideal red men. In the language of the Illinois Indians, the word *illinois* means "men"—"as if they looked upon all other Indians as beasts." The aborigines of Hayti believed that their island was the first of all things, that the sun and moon issued from one of its caverns, and men from another. Each Australian tribe, says Mr. Curr, regards its country as the centre of the earth, which in most cases is believed not to extend more than a couple of hundred miles or so in any direction. ... The Chinese are taught to think themselves superior to all other peoples. In their writings, ancient and modern, the word "foreigner" is regularly joined with some disrespectful epithet, implying or expressing the ignorance, brutality, obstinacy, or meanness of alien nations, and their obligations to or dependence upon China. To Confucius himself China was "the middle kingdom," "the multitude of great states," "all under heaven," beyond which were only rude and barbarous tribes. According to Japanese ideas, Nippon was the first country created, and the centre of the world. The ancient Egyptians considered themselves as the peculiar people, specially loved by the gods. They alone were termed "men" (romet); other nations were negroes, Asiatics, or Libyans, but not men; and according to the myth, these nations were descended from the enemies of the gods. The national pride of the Assyrians, so often referred to by the Hebrew prophets, is conspicuous everywhere in their cuneiform inscriptions: they are the wise, the brave, the powerful, who, like the deluge, carry away all resistance; their kings are the "matchless, irresistible"; and their gods are much exalted above the gods of all other nations. To the Hebrews, their own land was "an exceeding good land," "flowing with milk and honey," "the glory of all lands"; and its inhabitants were a holy people which the Lord had chosen "to be a special people unto Himself, above all people that are upon the face of the earth." Concerning the ancient Persians, Herodotus writes:—"They look upon themselves as very greatly superior in all respects to the rest of mankind, regarding others as approaching to excellence in proportion as they dwell nearer to them; whence it comes to pass that those who are the farthest off must be the most degraded of mankind." To this day, the monarch of Persia retains the title of "the Centre of the Universe"; and it is not easy to persuade a native of Isfahan that any European capital can be superior to his native city. The Greeks called Delphi—or rather the round stone in the Delphic temple—"the navel" or "middle point of the earth"; and they considered the natural relation between themselves and barbarians to be that between master and slave.

Evangelical, *n.* A Jesus fiend seeking to recruit new addicts.

Evildoer, *n.* Anyone who does anything.

Evolution, *n.* A theory that explains how dogs became Darwinian dogmatists.

Excommunicate, *v.* Formerly, to exclude from the Mass. Now, to exclude from the mass media.

Existence Exists, *phr.* A truism considered profound by those who do not understand that tautologies are tautological.

Existentialist, *n.* Sartre for Sartre's sake. One who believes the egg precedes the chicken.

Expectation, *n.* A prerequisite for disappointment.

Experience, *n.* A capricious teacher, often indulgent but sometimes extremely strict.

Exploration, *n.* A prelude to exploitation.

Extinct, *adj.* The present condition of a lifeform that was not fit to survive. For example, John F. Kennedy and several other Kennedys are now extinct. This proves they were not fit to survive, so good riddance to the dead Kennedys.

Extispicy, *n.* Happy entrails to you.

Extraterrestrial, *n.* A visitor from the space between someone's ears. What's that? You say that you have *personally* encountered an alien that did not come from inside your brain? Then perhaps it came from Uranus.

Eyewitness, *n.* One who sees things with his own eyes—then lies about them through his own teeth. One who said he saw something—and who is therefore competent to give false testimony about it.

Eyewitnesses have testified to having seen all of the following phenomena: elves; fairies; leprechauns; the resurrection and ascension of Jesus Christ; werewolves; vampires; ghosts; goblins; incubi; succubi; sailing ships in the clouds; flying saucers; spaceships; little green men; men in black; men from Mars; women from Venus; bleeding sacramental wafers flying through the air; witches flying through the air on broomsticks; the Blessed Virgin Mary hovering in the air; the Miracle of the Sun at Fatima; the Angel of Mons; the spectral soccer player of Amiens; forced conversions in Catholic nunneries; mass child molestations in daycare centers; Bigfoot; the Abominable Snowman; the Loch Ness Monster; N-rays; orgone energy; the Mad Gasser of Mattoon; the ritual murder of Christian children for their blood; the ritual murder of Jewish children by Nazis for their blood; geysers of blood spurting from mass graves for months after the Babi Yar massacre; the homicidal gas chambers of Treblinka; the homicidal steam chambers of Treblinka; Adolf Hitler riding in a Mercedes-Benz with Martin Borman in Miami Beach; and Joseph Mengele playing piano in a Latin-jazz combo in a nightclub in Los Angeles.

Fabian, *n.* A creeping socialist.

Facist, *n.* One who judges people on the basis of their face, just as a racist judges people on the basis of their race.

Fact, *n.* Something someone says exists or has occurred.

Fair Deal, *n.* Socialism with Truman's face.

Faith, *n.* The power by means of which a Christian can move a mountain, assuming he also uses some high explosives.

Faith Healer, *n.* A human placebo.

Fakir, *n.* One who has mastered the Indian rope-a-dope trick.

False Prophet, *n.* A prophet. Fake prophets (i.e., prophets) have included Isaiah, Jeremiah, Ezekial, Daniel, St. John the Insane, and Jesus H. Christ. Here's a false prophecy by Jesus, as reported in the Gospel According to Mark, 9:1 (and elsewhere):

> And he said unto them, Verily I say unto you, That there be some of them that stand here, which shall not taste of death, till they have seen the kingdom of God come with power.

Did any of Jesus' disciples live to see the "kingdom of God come with power?" Not that I know of.

Falsies, *n.*, *pl.* Two reasons why a skeptic might want to see things with his own eyes.

Fame, *n.* A flame that attracts moths in human form.

Fanatic, *n.* A barking dogmatist.

Farmer's Strike, *n.* Turning plowshares into swords, the better to plunder the consumer.

Fascinating, *adj.* In show business, faintly interesting.

Fedayeen, *n.* Those who sacrifice themselves and/or others.

Fellow Traveler, *n.* A running dog of the Communists.

Feminism, *n.* The doctrine that a woman has a right to one ball and half a cock—a half-cocked idea if I ever heard one. Of course, by the same token, a man should have a right to one tit and half a cunt.

Feminist, *n*. A Fondamentalist. A woman whose consciousness has gotten uppity. A sister who wants to be Big Brother. A bitch who wants to be top dog. A female-chauvinist sow, such as Andrea Dworkin (a porker in need of a good porking, but she won't get it from me). One who thinks the Isle of Man should be renamed the "Isle of Person."

Feyerabend, Paul, *n*. A philosopher of science who exposed the pauperism of Popperism.

Fireman, *n*. One who fights fires, sometimes after starting them.

Fireworks, *n*., *pl*. Weapons with which a patriot assaults the sensibilities of the indifferent. Every 4th of July, "the rockets red glare, the bombs bursting in air" give "proof thru the night" that patriotism is the last refuge of scoundrels intent on disturbing the peace.

First Amendment, *n*. An amendment to the Constitution of the United States forbidding Congress to interfere with the establishment of revisionism, the freedom to screech, the freedom to depress, or the right to peaceably dissemble.

Fish Liberation, *n*. Revolution for the halibut.

Flag-Burning, *n*. A form of symbolic speech protected by the First Amendment, like bra-burning, draft card–burning, cross-burning, book-burning, and Constitution-burning.

Flasher, *n.* An extropervert.

Flatterer, *n.* One who butters you up before devouring you.

Flower Power, *n.* A militant offshoot of the plant liberation movement.

Flying Saucers, *n., pl.* Saucers full of applesauce from outer space. Chariots of the frauds.

Fnord, *n.* The true living word of God.

Foreign Aid, *n.* A gift from one gang of thieves to another gang of thieves. Handouts across the sea.

Foreskin, *n.* A fold of skin that covers the glans of the penis, created by Yahweh to create work for mohels.

Fornication, *n.* Fucking without a license. Remember, fucking is not a right but a privilege granted by the state, a privilege which may be revoked if it is abused. Please refrain from reckless fucking at all times.

Fort, Charles Hoy, *n.* A man who committed the heresy of suggesting that meteors are not the only things that fall from the sky. Ironically, according to Martin Gardner's *Fads and Fallacies in the Name of Sciences*, belief in meteors was a scientific heresy in the 18th century.

Forties, The, *n.* The golden age of Hollywood, comic books, science fiction, and mass atrocity.

Founding Fathers, *n., pl.* The gods who created the United States. The Sacred Word of the Founding Fathers is to be found in the Declaration of Independence and the Constitution.

Fountainhead, *n.* The very best kind of head, the kind that Ayn Rand used to give to Nathaniel Branden.

Frank, Anne, *n.* For some, a substitute for the Virgin Mary.

Freedom, *n.* One's preferred form of slavery.

Freedom Fighter, *n.* A terrorist, such as Yasir Shamir or Yitzhak Arafat.

Free Love, *n.* Cheap sex.

Free Lunch, *n.* A barmecide feast.

Free Society, *n.* A libertarian utopia of total freedom, which will exist eternally in the future and never in the present.

Free Speech, *n.* Let a hundred idiots bloom! Remember, speech is free—for he who has a mouth (unless, of course, the cat or the state's got his tongue).

Freethinker, *n.* One who thinks he is free. A truthsucker.

Freethought Today, ***n.*** The same thing as freethought a century ago.

French Theory, *n.* Theory that has a funny accent and eats snails.

Fugu, _n._ A very poisonous fish, which the all-knowing creator-god Yahweh apparently didn't remember when He dictated dietary laws to Moses, for although the fugu is very poisonous, because it has scales and fins it is completely kosher. So Orthodox Jews should feel free to eat fugu.

Fukuyama, Francis, _n._ A Hegelian guru who held that history is history.

Full-Figure Girl, _n._ An aging actress with big boobs.

Fundamentalist, _n._ In Christianity, one who believes that all statements in the Bible should be taken literally, as distinguished from a biblical liberal, who believes that some such statements should be taken with a grain of salt. As for myself, I take all biblical statements with a _pillar_ of salt.

Futurism, _n._ In art, a wave of the past.

Futurologist, _n._ A prophet not inspired by God who nonetheless turns out to be wrong just as often as prophets inspired by God.

Gaffe, *n.* A goof. In political discourse, a gaffe often consists in telling the truth.

Gameshow Contestant, *n.* One who knows the price of everything and the value of nothing.

Garden of Eden, The, *n.* An early nudist camp.

Gas Oven, *n.* In Holocaust lore, the hybrid offspring of a gas chamber and a crematory oven. A mythical creature sometimes said to have existed in certain of the Nazi concentration camps.

Gastronomic, *adj.* Of or pertaining to the production of gas.

Gawad, *n.* The name given to the Supreme Being by Southern preachers.

Gay, *adj.* Happy—in a queer sort of way.

Gay Day, *n.* St. Vaseline's Day.

Gay Liberationist, *n.* One who has forgotten that forbidden fruit is the sweetest.

GBLT, *n.* A BLT sandwich with guacamole.

Generalize, *v.* In general, lies.

Genius, *n.* The genie in us.

Genteel, *adj.* Gentile.

Genuflect, *v.* To perform a knee bend as part of a religious exercise.

German, *n.* The source of German measles.

Ghetto, *n.* Ashanti town.

Ghost, *n.* *Esprit de corpse.*

Glossolalia, *n.* Speech which gains in originality what it loses in intelligibility. The Holy Babble.

God, *n.* The Biggest Wheel in the Head. The Supreme Spook. According to Jeff Riggenbach, Orson Welles was God. However, when once presented with the assertion that if Orson Welles was God, then God would not be omniscient, Riggenbach replied that he had never affirmed the omniscience of God, only His omnipresence.

Goddess, *n.* A dickless deity with holy hooters and a paradisiacal pussy.

God-Fearing, *adj.* Scared of the sacred. Afraid of nothing.

God-Given, *adj.* Given by an Indian giver (the Lord giveth, and the Lord taketh away), as, for example, our God-given, inalienable rights.

God's Law, *n.* Man's law revealed through smoke and mirrors to overawe the rubes.

Gold Bug, *n.* One who proclaims, "Ingots we trust."

Gonzo Journalist, *n.* An amuckracker.

Good Citizen, *n.* An obedient slave.

Good Guy, *n.* A type of character found exclusively in works of fiction.

Good News, *n.* In Christianity, the news that possibly, just possibly, God might decide not to torture you in Hell for all eternity if you can correctly figure out which of the 999 different denominations of Christianity is the one and only one you must join in order to be saved.

Good Samaritan, *n.* A dead Samaritan.

Good Sex, *n.* Sex with someone other than Dr. Ruth.

Good Will, *n.* A will that leaves me a lot of money. According to Kant, "a good will is the only thing that is good in and of itself."

Gore, *n.* The lifeblood of patriotism.

Gospel, *n.* The Tallest Tale Ever Told. A work of Golgothic fiction. The Cruci-fiction.

Government, *n.* A glorified gang.

Government of Laws, *n.* Government by lawyers.

Goy, *n.* An unchosen person. A gentile.

According to "Avner," author of *Memoirs of an Assassin: Confessions of a Stern Gang Killer*:

> For the European Jew, the term is not necessarily one of abuse. It is the way in which it is said which gives it its character. For the Lehi [Stern Gang], on the other hand, an Englishman would always be a filthy Goy, who could be killed for this reason alone....

Oy! It's hard to be a goy!

Grandiloquence, *n.* Bombastardized speech or style.

Gray Matter, *n.* The type of matter necessary for discerning shades of gray rather than seeing things in black and white. Gray matter is not the matter with Kansas.

Great Communicator, The, *n.* A second-rate actor. He who awe-shucks and jives.

Greatest Generation, *n.* A generation of vipers.

Great Society, *n.* America after it went all the way with LBJ. In short, America the Fucked.

Greenbacker, *n.* A member of the former US political party that wished to leave the legal issue of money to the tender mercies of the government.

Greenbacks, *n.* Illegal immigrants from Ireland.

Greenspan, *n.* The width of a handful of Federal Reserve Notes.

Grenada, *n.* Ronald Reagan's greatest hour— and I mean that *literally*.

Gullible, *adj.* Capable of being a gull, such as Jonathan Livingston Seagull.

Guru, *n.* In the mysterious East, a teacher or guide, especially one dealing in religious, spiritual, and/or financial matters.

Gush Emunim, *n.* A group of devout landgrabbers.

Hack, *n.* A writer whose only muse is Mammon.

Halal, *adj.* Kosher for Koran-thumpers.

Hallucination, *n.* Every nation. An apparent perception of something not actually present. For example, if you look at an egg frying in a pan but think you see your brain on drugs, that is a hallucination.

Hamas, *n.* Israel's Frankenstein monster? (It has been alleged that in the late 1980s, Israel supported Hamas in order to weaken Arafat's Fatah.)

Hammer, *n.* A tool used to hit nails, such as fingernails and thumbnails.

Happiness, *n.* A wild goose, disguised as a

bluebird, which everyone has an inalienable right to chase.

Hardcore Pornography, *n.* Pornography which makes one's core hard.

Hate Group, *n.* A group that you are encouraged to hate.

Hate Literature, *n.* Literature which I hate—for example, Elie Wiesel's essay "Appointment With Hate," included in his book *Legends of Our Time* (1970). In this essay, Wiesel writes,

> After the war, I had deliberately avoided contact with all Germans. Their presence sickened me physically. The blood rushed to my head whenever I received a letter from a cousin in Frankfurt. Where Germany was concerned, logical arguments no longer had any force....

> There is a time to love and a time to hate; whoever does not hate when he should does not deserve to love when he should, does not deserve to love when he is able.... Every Jew, somewhere in his being, should set apart a zone of hate—healthy, virile hate—for what the German personifies and for what persists in the German.

Heathenism, *n.* Any practice deemed illegitimate by a monotonotheist. The ecclesiastical statutes of King Edgar of England (959 AD) thus directed

> that every priest zealously promote Christianity, and totally extinguish every heathenism; and forbid well worshippings, and necromancies, and divinations, and enchantments, and man worshippings, and the vain practices which are carried on with various spells, and with frith-

splots, and with elders and also with various other trees, and with stozes, and with many various delusions, with which men do much of what they should not.

Heaven, _n._ A place where dead Christians will be happy forever. The Reverend Billy Graham has said that he expects to be able to play golf in Heaven, because Heaven has everything one needs to be happy. The Reverend Graham has also said that there is no sex in Heaven. Draw your own conclusions, brethren.

Heavy Metal Band, _n._ A lightweight musical ensemble.

Hedonism, _n._ A doctrine holding that the pleasure of hedonists is the highest good.

Hell, _n._ God's gulag. A Dachau for the damned, created by Our Führer Who Art in Heaven. A cosmic concentration camp for metaphysical criminals and dissidents.

Hello, _interj._ Welcome to Hell. (See Sartre's _No Exit._)

Hemlock, _n._ The cure for philosophy.

Hemophilia, _n._ A disorder in which blood both is and is not thicker than water.

Heresy, _n._ Cognitive dissidence. An underdogma.

In Christianity, heresy signifies disagreement with the One True Lie. In a sermon dating to around 1260 AD, Bertold of Regensburg expressed his aversion to heresy in these moderate terms:

> If I had a brother, I would rather that he had slain a hundred men than that he were in a single heresy. I would rather that my sister had had a hundred men, and that my brother had slain all his children with his own hand.

Heretic, *n.* A brazen Hussite.

Hero, *n.* A man of exceptional courage, fortitude, or bold enterprise. For example, The Deranged Loner. ("Say, who was that man in the dark glasses?" "I don't know, but he left behind this exploding bullet and a photo of Jodie Foster." And as we see him riding out of town on the bus, the *William Tell Overture* begins to play as the Deranged Loner leans his head out of the window and yells, "Hi–Yo, Greyhound!")

Heroin, *n.* The Hitler of drugs.

Hierarchy, *n.* Rule by Rabbi Marvin Hier. Today, the Simon Wiesenthal Center. Tomorrow, the world!

According to Gary Rosenblatt, editor of the *Baltimore Jewish Times*, Rabbi Hier

> says he felt from the beginning that the ideal site for a Holocaust museum would be a yeshiva because it would offer living proof that Judaism had survived Hitler. "What's the ultimate memorial to the six million? That Torah lives on, that the Jewish people live on," says the rabbi. "Our memorial is against assimilation. It stands for the future destiny of the Jewish people. It is not a cold memorial of bricks and mortar but a place where students carry out God's command to be

> vigilant against Amalek (the biblical personification of Israel's enemies). That's the lesson of the Holocaust... We see ourselves as an Orthodox institution not happy with the image that Orthodox institutions must be limited to narrow religious issues. We're not like that. We operate on every front. We will speak up whenever and wherever Jews are put on the defensive. Our goal is to work for *Am Yisrael* (the people of Israel) and be involved in all issues affecting Jews...."

The State of California is now [circa 1986] subsidizing the expansion of the Simon Wiesenthal Center's "Museum of Tolerance," which, says Rabbi Hier, is "against assimilation" and "stands for the future destiny of the Jewish people." And only one state legislator had the nerve to vote against this righteous, rabbinical rip-off of California's taxpayers.

Higher Truth, The, *n.* The truth that is over my head.

Hiroshima Revisionism, *n.* Enola Gay–bashing.

Historical Jesus, The, *n.* Any alleged actual Jesus, as distinct from any theologized Jesus. There are now 47,693 different theories about "the historical Jesus." The current favorite of this illustrious lexicographer is the theory that "the historical Jesus" was a poached egg. (See C. S. Lewis, *Mere Christianity*.)

Hitler, Adolf, *n.* The anti-Semitic messiah. Ironically, however, Hitler himself was Jewish. His real name: Adolf Shekelgrubber. How do I know this? I myself am his son, Shecky Shekelgrubber.

Hofmann, Albert, *n.* The Wonderful Wizard of Sandoz.

Holiday, *n.* A day set aside for the celebration of getting off work or out of school.

Holocaust, The, *n.* A holocaust. A smokescreen obscuring the atrocities of the Allies and the Israelis. The hallucinogenocide. The insurance fraud of the century. A cheap cinematic trick; a flim-flam; the Hollywoodcaust; a soap opera; *The Greatest Sob Story Ever Told* (*With a Cast of Millions!*).

Did you see *The Wall*, the TV movie about the Warsaw ghetto? If so, then you may recall that after the deportation of Jews from Warsaw began, the character played by Tom Conti followed a train carrying Jews to Treblinka. There he saw a crematory building with huge chimneys spewing black clouds of smoke into the sky. Thus he learned that Jews were being murdered at Treblinka.

But this is an example of what is known as "dramatic license." In reality, Zalman Friedrich, who supposedly followed a train carrying Jews out of Warsaw, never claimed to have gone all the way to Treblinka but only to a town near the camp. There he supposedly met an escapee from Treblinka, who supposedly told him that Jews were being murdered there.

Furthermore, there was no crematory building at Treblinka, no chimneys spewing clouds of black smoke. At the time in question, the Jews allegedly murdered there were allegedly buried in mass graves, not cremated.

Finally, even if there had been a crematory building there, as there was at Auschwitz-Birkenau, the chimneys would not have been spewing clouds of smoke into the air. The patent of Topf and Son, the builders of the Auschwitz-Birkenau crematories, indicates that it was impossible for them to emit smoke. And this seems to be confirmed by the aerial photographs of Auschwitz-Birkenau published in the CIA monograph *The Holocaust Revisited* (1979). According to the two CIA photo interpreters who analyzed the aerial photos taken of Auschwitz-Birkenau between April 1944, and January 1945, "Although survivors recalled that smoke and flame emanated continually from the crematoria chimneys and was visible for miles, the photography we examined gave no positive proof of this." In other words, *none* of the aerial photos of Auschwitz-Birkenau show *any* smoke or flame coming from the crematoria chimneys.

Are you a believer in the infallibility of eyewitness testimony of Holocaust survivors? If so, then I suggest you look at the aerial photographs of Auschwitz-Birkenau, and then ask yourself if you believe Holocaust survivors or your own eyes.

Holocaust Denier, *n.* A dirty, rotten rat bastard who denies the overwhelming evidence (see "Overwhelming Evidence") that the Nazis killed six million Jews. For example, this illustrious lexicographer is a Holocaust denier who asserts that six million Jews faked their own deaths as part of a massive insurance fraud scheme.

Holocaust Literature, *n.* An increasingly popular subgenre of horror fiction. Grim fairy tales.

One of the most entertaining examples of Holocaust literature is Filip Mueller's *Eyewitness Auschwitz: Three Years in the Gas Chambers* (1979). Here is just one of Mueller's many tales from the crematoria:

> From time to time, SS doctors visited the crematorium, above all *Haupsturmfuehrer* Kitt and *Oberscharfuehrer* Weber. During the visits it was just like working in a slaughterhouse. Like cattle dealers they felt the calves and thighs of men and women who were still alive and selected what they called the best pieces before the victims were executed. After their execution, the chosen bodies were laid on a table. The doctors proceeded to cut pieces of still warm flesh from the thighs and calves and threw them into waiting receptacles. The muscles of those who had been shot were still working and contracting, making the bucket jump about."

Got that? Made the "bucket jump about"?

What a story, eh? Cinematic as hell. Why Hollywood hasn't given the Mueller memoirs the movie treatment is beyond me. Tobe Hooper could direct, or maybe George Romero. Of course, Hollywood being what it is, it would take some liberties with the story.

Picture this: A bucket chock full of chunks of pulsating human flesh is jumping around on the floor of the Auschwitz crematorium like a frog in a fry pan. Nazi doctors frantically pursue the bucket as it hops out the door and makes for the electrified fence surrounding the camp. Dodging bursts of machine gun fire, the jumping bucket soars over the fence with a mighty leap into freedom. It escapes to neutral Switzerland and tries to alert humanity to the atrocities of Auschwitz. But a cynical world does not believe the *eyewitness* testimony of the jumping bucket. The horror of Auschwitz is not stopped, and the disillusioned flesh pot leaps to its death from a snowy alpine peak.

Another entertaining example of Holocaust literature is Martin Gray's *For Those I Loved* (1971), a hair-raising account of the author's experiences during the Holocaust, including his imprisonment at Treblinka, where he was forced to carry corpses from gas chambers to mass graves.

Gray's book was favorably reviewed by *Books for Libertarians*. It was a Book-of-the-Month Club selection, and Gilbert Highet told *Book-of-the-Month Club News* readers that it is "a story stranger and wilder than any fiction you have ever read." A review in the San Francisco Chronicle proclaimed it to be "as exciting as anything since *Papillon*."

No wonder. According to British journalist Gitta Sereny,

> Gray's *For Those I Loved* was the work of Max

Gallo the ghostwriter, who also produced *Papillon*. During the research for a *Sunday Times* inquiry into Gray's work, M. Gallo informed me coolly that he "needed" a long chapter on Treblinka because the book required something strong for pulling in readers. When I myself told Gray, the "author," that he had manifestly never been to, nor escaped from Treblinka, he finally asked, despairingly, "But does it matter?" Wasn't the only thing that Treblinka *did* happen, that it *should* be written about, and that some Jews should be shown to have been heroic? (*New Statesman*, 2 November 1979)

Holocaust Revisionism, *n.* Historiographic pornography. A thoughtcrime against humanity; the intellectual equivalent of Zyklon B. For example, one Fortean Holocaust revisionist believes that the six million Jews of Europe were burned to death not by the Nazis but by spontaneous combustion. Another believes that the Nazis actually shipped the six million Jews to Miami as part of a massive resettlement program—but that they all mysteriously disappeared without a trace while sailing through the Bermuda Triangle. I myself believe that Holocaust revisionism is such an obscenity that Holocaust revisionists should have their mouths washed out with soap made from the fat of murdered Jews.

Holocaust Revisionist, *n.* One who denies that he is a denier.

Holocaust Satire, *n.* A literary form of playing with fire.

Holocaust Studies, *n*. Education by Zionist comprachicos.

Holocaust Survivor, *n*. A blues singer whose signature song is "Nobody Knows the Treblinka I've Seen." A Semitic saint who would never ever tell a lie, not in a million, not even in six million years.

Holy Father, The, *n*. The head of a church that worships Jesus, who reportedly said, "Call no man on Earth your father." (Matthew 23:9)

Holy Ghost, The, *n*. The poltergeist that banged the Virgin Mary and knocked her up.

Holy Grail, The, *n*. A holy cup or stone or bloodline or something. At any rate, whatever it is exactly, it's holy.

Holy War, *n*. A war, for God's sake.

Holy Writ, *n*. Sacred bullshit.

Home, *n*. A utopian paradise of peace, comfort, cheer, and love. There is no place like home.

Homocaust, The, *n*. The Nazi extermination of the queers.

Homophobia, *n*. An irrational fear and hatred of homos.

Homosexual, *n*. A man's man who is not a ladies' man.

Homosexuality, *n*. Formerly, the love that dare not speak its name. Now, the love that does dare shriek its euphemistic Newspeak pseudonym.

Honest Politician, *n.* A politician who steals no more than is legally allowed.

Honesty, *n.* The best policy for liars.

Honorable, *adj.* A formal title of courtesy for certain disreputable officials.

Hoover, J. Edgar, *n.* A vacuum cleaner that sucked up lots of dirt.

Hope, *n.* The eternal deceiver. (For details, see H.L. Mencken's essay "The Cult of Hope," or see my forthcoming book, *The Mendacity of Hope*.)

Hophead, *n.* A narcotics addict, especially an opium addict. This name makes no sense since it is beer, not narcotics, that is made with hops.

Horah, *n.* An Israeli folk dance. I wonder: Were the five dancing Israelis who were arrested on 9/11 dancing the horah? And is it illegal to dance the horah in New Jersey? Is that why they were arrested?

Horny, *adj.* Having romance in one's pants.

Hostage, *n.* A terrorist or other criminal's detainee.

Houri, *n.* In Islamic belief, harpie in the sky.

Housekeeper, *n.* The one who keeps the house after a divorce.

House of Representatives, *n.* A house that is usually divided against itself and yet still stands. A house of ill repute.

Humanitarian, *n.* One whose diet consists entirely of humans.

Humanitarian Intervention, *n.* The killing of some people, ostensibly to prevent the killing of some people.

Human Resources, *n., pl.*, People fit for exploitation.

Human Rights, *n., pl.* Rights deserved by all humans (but not by beasts in human form, such as myself).

Hun, *n.* A term of endearment, formerly used in reference to our good friends the Krauts.

Hunting, *n.* A crime against animality, except in the case of hunting humans.

Hurricane, *n.* An act of God, which proves that God is a terrorist, an evildoer who should be hunted down and killed like a mad dog.

Hush Money, *n.* The reason why silence is golden.

Huxley, Aldous, *n.* A writer notorious for his virulent anti-Semitism, as expressed in such books as *Eyeless in Gaza* and *Brave Jew World*.

Hymn, *n.* A song to Him. Here is an example of a hymn:

> *My Lord Jesus, You've healed the cripples.*
> *You're more delicious than a young girl's nipples.*
> *My Lord Jesus, You make my heart throb.*
> *If you really love me, you'll give me a blowjob.*

Hypocracy, *n.* Rule by hypocrites, the only form of government there is. In the US, each of the major political parties accuses the other of hypocrisy, and both are correct in that accusation.

Hypocrite, *n.* One who practices vice while preaching versa. A human being.

Iconoclast, *n.* An axiom murderer.

Ideal, *adj.* I deal.

Idealist, *n.* One who has noble, altruistic reasons for wanting to slaughter people.

Identity Christian, *n.* Fake-identity Christian.

Ideologist, *n.* One who has made his Procrustean bed and now must lie in it.

Ideologue, *n.* A doctrinaire-head.

Ideology, *n.* A substitute for thinking. Idiotology.

Idiot, *n.* Anyone who disagrees with an asshole.

I Do, *phr.* Adieu—to freedom.

Ignoramus, *n.* One who only knows what he

reads in the papers.

Immaculate Conception, *n.* The ideal mental state, in which one conceives only immaculate thoughts concerning the Virgin Mary. A mental state usually attained by brainwashing.

Immoralist, *n.* One who cannot feel guilt with a clear conscience.

Immortalist, *n.* An optimist who isn't dead yet. One who intends to live forever, such as Robert Anton Wilson (January 18, 1932 – January 11, 2007) or Timothy Leary (October 22, 1920 – May 31, 1996).

Impeachment, *n.* In the United States, the House of Pots presenting formal charges of blackness against a kettle on the federal stove. This is a Constitutional requirement for the removal of the kettle from its burner.

Impiety, *n.* The piety of an imp.

Inbred, *adj.* Having ancestors who were incestors.

Incest Survivor, *n.* One of the rare few victims of incest who has lived to tell the tale to Oprah.

Incorruptible, *adj.* Overpriced.

Indisputable, *adj.* That which cannot be disputed, according to someone who doesn't want it disputed.

Individual, *n.* The smallest of all minorities, frequently ganged up on by minority groups.

Individualism, *n.* A doctrine antithetical to individuality, though it is the least unrealistic form of collectivism. The form of conformism predominant in America.

Indochina War, *n.* American youth in Asia.

Induct, *v.* Abduct.

Inevitable, *adj.* Unavoidable, unless you do what I tell you to do to avoid it.

In Fact, *phr.* In someone's unproven assertion.

Infallible, *adj.* Incapable of admitting error.

Inferiority Complex, *n.* A lowlier-than-thou attitude.

Informed Sources, n, *pl.* Sources who say they are informed.

Ingrate, *n.* A person not properly appreciative of benefits received, such as one who looks a Trojan horse in the mouth.

Inhuman, *adj.* Human but disapproved.

Innocent Victim, *n.* The best kind of victim for propaganda purposes. After all, who would care about a guilty victim?

Intellectual, *n.* One who thinks (what someone else has already thought).

Intellectual Activist, *n.* One who supports reason—with all his heart. An ineffectual activist.

Intellectual Ammunition, *n.* Verbal bullets

for Objectivists who want to shoot their mouths off. Blank-out cartridges.

International Community, *n.* Me, my friends, and my stooges.

Internet, The, *n.* The information, misinformation, and disinformation superhighway.

Intuition, *n.* A means of acquiring knowledge without paying tuition.

Investigative Journalism, *n.* A passing fad of the 1970s.

Investor, *n.* One who gambles on Wall Street rather than in Atlantic City or Las Vegas.

Invisible Hand, The, *n.* A hand that's giving most people the finger.

Iran, *n.* A country ruled by mullahs, as distinguished from the USA, which is ruled by moolah.

Iraq War, *n.* President George W. Bush's last choice. Unfortunately, also his first choice.

Ireland, *n.* The land of ire.

Irrefutable Evidence, *n.* In State Department propaganda, evidence that cannot be refuted because it cannot be examined.

An equivalent expression, "unimpeachable evidence," has been employed by the Palestinian Arab propagandist Issah Nakleh in his "Memorandum to the President," published in *The Journal of Historical Review* (Fall 1982). According to Nakleh,

> The proof that Egypt was not prepared or preparing for the war is the fact that, in the evening of June 4, 1967, a party was held for the airforce graduates in Anshas (former Farouk palace and gardens), where practically every important officer in the Egyptian airforce and all its commanders were present in that party until the early hours of the morning of June 5, when the Israelis attacked at 4 a.m. According to unimpeachable evidence in our possession, Egyptian agents of the Israeli Intelligence were able to put LSD in the drinks and coffee served to most important officers and top command of the Egyptian airforce. When Israeli airplanes struck at 4 a.m. on the morning of June 5, most of the Egyptian airforce officers were asleep and incapacitated by LSD. We have also unimpeachable evidence that the Israeli airplanes dropped LSD-25, a nerve gas, on Egyptian forces. These facts prove that the Israeli armed forces won the 1967 war by deception, conspiracy, and using the LSD-25 nerve gas.

Nakleh has never revealed the "unimpeachable evidence" for this tale of Israeli intrigue, and I do not believe it for two reasons. First, when I take LSD. in the evening, I am unable to get to sleep by 4 a.m. the next morning. Second, LSD-25 is not a nerve gas; it is simply a slightly more precise designation for LSD If Issah Nakleh actually has "unimpeachable evidence" to back up his accusations, I'll hump a camel.

IRS, *n.* The Black Hand at the end of the long arm of the law. The real Stark Fist of Removal.

Islam, *n.* Submission—to a dead camelfucker (piss be upon him).

Islamic Republic, *n.* A misrepresentative theocracy. An Allahgarchy.

Islamist, *n.* One who performs literary criticism not with a pen but with a scimitar.

Islamofascist, *n.* A Muslim follower of Mussolini. One who believes in the Koran and the corporate state. In short, a figment of the imagination of the Zionazi.

Islamophobia, *n.* Irrational fear and hatred of Islam, as distinguished from the rational fear and hatred of Islam, for which there is no word.

Isolationist, *n.* A selfish bastard who stubbornly doesn't want to be bothered with slaughtering foreigners.

Israel, *n.* A nation built with guns, guts, guile, and guilt. Eretz Peretz. The last refuge of a Jewish scoundrel. The Zion Curtain country. An itsy-bitsy, teeny-weeny, tiny little nation surrounded by enemies, especially the Mediterranean Sea, a virulently anti-Semitic body of water just waiting for a chance to drown the Jews. The United States' best ally in the Middle East, which is why whenever the US gets into a war in the Middle East, Israeli troops are right there, fighting along with American troops against our common foes. Israel has a right to exist. Indeed, it is the only nation in the Middle East that has such a right.

Israeli Citizen, *n.* One who lives in the Jewish state, i.e., a state of paranoia.

J

Jackson, Andrew, *n.* A US president who re-putedly was a Freemason and, therefore, must have been a tool of the Bankers' Conspiracy. Or maybe not.

Jahmaica, *n.* The original home of the Rastafari movement.

Jailer, *n.* One who is his brother's keeper.

Jehovah's Witnesses, *n., pl.* Those who bear witness to God's wish to be known as "Jehovah" and not "God," "Yahweh," "Allah," or "Elvis." All I know about this is that when I was God's right-hand man and close personal friend, I always called him "Goddy."

Jesuitical, *adj.* Casuistical.

Jesus, *n.* The light of the world, a light so bright that believers in Jesus are blinded. The imaginary friend of over a billion children of all ages. A false prophet, according to the Gospel of Mark. (See Mark 8:38-9:1.) The sin of God. The Meshugah.

Jesuszilla, *n.* The Son of Godzilla and the Virgin Maryzilla.

Jewish Defense League, *n.* The Kosher Kikes Klan. One of their terror tactics is the burning of a Star of David on the lawns of uppity gentiles.

Jewish Settlement, *n.* A type of settlement precluding a Jewish–Arab settlement.

Joke, *n.* Something said to amuse, such as the following:

Q: How do queer Boy Scouts start a fire?
A: They rub two dicks together.

Q: What does a Zionist say after sex?
A: "Was it good for the Jews?"

According to Harvey B. Schechter of the Anti-Defamation League (or Harvey B. Sphincter of the Anti-Defecation League, as I sometimes think of him), "there are some things about which one doesn't or shouldn't make jokes. The Holocaust is one of them." Following is one of the Holocaust jokes that Harvey published in order to show the kind of joke that shouldn't be published: "What's the difference between a Jew and a pizza? A pizza doesn't scream when you put it in the oven."

Jonah, *n.* The protagonist of a biblical fish story. In this case, however, the one that got away was the man and not the fish. I find the story much harder to swallow than the fish allegedly did Jonah.

Jones, Alex, *n.* A drama queen. A bullshitter with a bullhorn. David Rockefeller's illegitimate grandson. There's something happening, and you don't know what it is, do you, Mr. Jones?

Jonestown, *n.* Utopia.

Joshua, *n.* A holy war criminal. According to the Old Testament, the Hittites, the Amorites, the Canaanites, the Perizzites, the Hivites, and the Jebusites were all marked out for total destruction by the Lord God of Israel:

> And so Joshua defeated the whole land, the hill country and the Negeb and the lowland and the slopes, and all their kings; he left none remaining, but utterly destroyed all that breathed, as the Lord God of Israel commanded.
> (Josh. 10:40, Revised Standard Version)

Journalism, *n.* One of the 555 ways of lying for a living. As John Fletcher wrote in *Wit Without Money* (1974), "Ask how to live? Write, write, write anything; The world's a fine believing world, write news!"

In "Why Media People Are and Should Be Liberals," Chapter 22 of *The Media in America* (1974), John Tebbel, a journalist and journalism professor, wrote,

> as for journalism students, there is no need for

indoctrination [to turn them into liberals]. They usually have the sharpest, most inquiring minds in the student body and like most journalists from the beginning of the profession, they seem to come equipped with a kind of innate resistance to humbug, a sensory apparatus which informs them that the world is full of people who are solemnly trying to tell them things that aren't so.

Of course, the world is full of people who are trying to tell journalists and journalism students things that aren't so—and John Tebbel is one of them.

Journalist, *n.* One of the *real* newsmakers. One who covers up the news. A liar for hire.

Joy Veh, *interj.* A Jewish expression of happiness.

Jungian, *n.* One who is a Freud of his own shadow.

Junior College, *n.* In California, an institution of hire education, in which one may major in such vocations as aviation wielding, inhalation therapy, or turf-grass management. High school with ash trays.

Just, *adj.* Just as I want.

Justice, *n.* A state of affairs in which some people are sent to prison for writing bad checks, while, for the same offense, David Mogulman is sentenced to make a movie.

Justification, *n.* Mystification. Just a fixation.

Just War, *n.* Merely war.

Ka'bah, *n.* The structure that houses the Black Stone, which is the only idol Muslims still worship.

Kabbalah, *n.* A possible source of tricky gnosis.

Kabbalist, *n.* A Jew who believes in Ayn Sof rather than Ayn Rand.

Kahanism, *n.* Hitlerism with a Hebrew face. Nazism with a hooked nose.

Are you one of those who repeatedly preach that those who forget the past are condemned to repeat it; that Hitler started out with a tiny following but, within a decade, became dictator of Germany; that Hitler had clearly revealed his evil intentions in *Mein Kampf*, but people either did not read it or did not believe what they read; and that such a tragedy as Hitlerism must never be allowed to happen again? If so, then have you read the writings of Rabbi Meir Kahane, founder of the Jewish Defense League and leader of Israel's Kach party?

Here, for example, are some choice quotations from Kahane's book *Forty Years* (1983):

> So let the watchman cry out the alarm and let the horn sound out the warning. For there is a G-d in the universe and He has made it and all that inhabit it. And He decrees that which shall be and all was made for a purpose, His purpose, the doing of His will. And a world that refuses to know Him must crumble and be shattered. (p. 14)

> And so, the Jew sits. Sits with all the others, the strangers, the foreigners, the gentiles, from whom he is bid to separate himself....
> The Jew waits. He waits to be a victim, twice over. Refusing to leave the graveyard that is the very nature of the Galut-Exile, he waits, unknowingly, to perish in it, G-d forbid. The Al-Mighty prepares the cup of retribution for the arrogance and heresy of the gentile .... (p.25)

> A world war becomes inevitable and its price is measured in billions of lives. The World-Exile stands on the precipice, moving immutably towards a war of fire that will exterminate nations and decimate lands. And all of this must be ....
> It is inevitable. And it is, too, the vow of an angry G-d of Israel, against the nations who know Him not and who, thus, contemptuously mangle His people Israel. It is the fury of a L-rd, G-d of Israel, whose name is forever linked to that of His people and who is humiliated and desecrated through the degradation of Israel. (pp.27–29)

> *The Jews against the Hellenists*. The real struggle. The dream of materialism fill (sic) the streets

and the acrid smell of yearning for pleasure assails the nostrils. In the parlor, on the bus, in the cafe, the talk is of money and what it can buy. The gentile world of magical sensualism and gratification of desires fills the bowels with a painful need and the holiness of Israel is exchanged for the dream of pagan America.

The reality becomes a land whose music rocks to gentile beat and rolls to the depths of ugly violence. Values that raised the Jew to but a little lower than the angels, are exchanged for those so base that he plunges lower than the beast. Judaism loses all meaning and Jewishness follows it into the junkheap of antiquity as Zionism becomes a word of mockery and cynicism. It is a land that raises its eyes unto the gentile films and televised pornography and cheers its pagan heroes even as it worships at the feet of uncircumcized basketball foreigners. Sinai is cast away for Times Square and the purity of the Chosen · people is exchanged for the material vomit of Los Angeles. The modesty of holiness is contemptuously abandoned and the nation wallows in the nakedness of gentile culture. (pp. 39–40)

Jewishness, not neo-Hellenism. Holiness, not the vomit of gentilization.

Life and the world itself were not created for equal tolerance of ideas be they good or evil, nor is the decision as to what is good or evil determined by majority rule. Life was created, the universe brought into being, in order to be pure and holy and good. There is no room in such a world for evil and impurity and the profane. A world made by He who is all good and pure cannot tolerate the antithesis of Him within it. And the Jew who is the chosen servant-messenger of the Al-Mighty in this world is commanded to eradicate and destroy and remove evil from the world of good. (p. 72)

And there is yet another aspect to the world of G-d for the Jew. It involves the fundamental commandment that is truly national in scope applying to the nation as a whole. It is the national mission of the Jew! It is the national mission to glorify the name of the L-rd among the nations of the world, to force them to "know Him," to have the entire world recognize that the L-rd is G-d, there is no other beside Him. For this was the world created, for this was Israel chosen. (p. 73)

The Name of the L-rd is irrevocably connected to that of His people Israel. And so is His shame. Jewish weakness, in the eyes of the gentile, is the weakness of the G-d of the Jews. And so, every Jewish national retreat, defeat, humil-iation, degradation, is seen in the eyes of the nations as the retreat, defeat, humiliation, deg-radation, AND NONEXISTENCE of the G-d of Israel. Jewish power, victory, trampling the high places of the enemy is the power and victory and EXISTENCE of the L-rd as the true, the One G-d. Only through His power and victory will the nations prostrate themselves in awe and cry out: The L-rd is G-d!" (p.75)

Kamikaze, *n.* A divine wind that blew some Americans away during World War II.

Karma, *n.* In order to explain this profound and significant metaphysical concept, I believe I can do no better than to let speak Joseph Donelly, spiritualist seer and healer:

What is Karmic-Law? It is the law of progress and, in spirit, it never ends. I was told once of my prior existence an "anmon" ago (1 million x 1 million x 1 million years). There are enough worlds in eternity so that everyone who was ever born can, in time, and after millions of incarna-tions, rise to the status of overseer of a particu-lar world. It truly staggers the imagination.

Kennedy, Ted, *n.* A bridge over troubled water.

Khan, Chaka, *n.* The chocolate Dolly Parton.

Khomeinikaze, *n.* A Shi'ite suicide bomber.

Kimchi, *n.* Seoul food.

King of Kings, The, *n.* The Boss of All Bosses.

Klansman, *n.* A white Muslin.

Klansperson, *n.* A racist who is not a sexist.

Knockers, *n.* A woman's breasts. Unfortunately, however, some women do not have knockers, only doorbells.

Knowledge, *n.* Justified true belief, as distinguished from unjustified true belief or justified untrue belief.

Koch, Ilsa, *n.* A fun-loving German lass who used to liven the party by putting a lampshade over her head.

Koran, The, *n.* A holy source of toilet paper, like the Bible, the Talmud, The Book of Mormon, The Urantia Book, etc. The Koran is also good for children's games of "kick the Koran." The Koran is the most beautiful book in the world—according to those who have never read another book. (Why not pick up a copy of *Pale Fire* by Nabokov, you ignorant camel jockeys?)

Label, *v.* To libel.

Labor Union, *n.* An association of workers organized to advance the interests of the union organizers.

Lady Godiva, *n.* The perfect role model for liberated women.

Lahaye, Tim, *n.* A premillenial dipsensation-alist who makes real profits by lying about false prophets.

Land Reform, *n.* The redistribution of dirt.

LaRouchite, *n.* A dope opposed to DOPE.

Las Vegans, *n., pl.* Hispanics who prefer their chili *sin carne*.

Late, *adj.* Not on time, sometimes because of being dead.

Lavon Affair, The, *n.* The political scandal in Israel that resulted from the failure of an Israeli conspiracy in Egypt. The conspiracy, Operation Susannah, involved Egyptian Jews who were working for Israel planting firebombs in US and British buildings in Cairo in 1954, intending to blame the bombings on Arab terrorists and sour relations between Egypt, on the one hand, and the U.S. and Britain, on the other. This is just one of the many reasons why Israel is so widely regarded as the US's best and most reliable ally in the Middle East.

Law, *n.* The preferred weapon of (some) robbers.

Law and Order, *n.* The political goal of getting criminals off the streets and back into public office, where they belong.

Lawyer, *n.* An attorney at large. Warning: All lawyers are armed with dangerous weapons—their tongues—and many of them are masters of the court-martial arts of tongue fu and Jewjitsu.

LDS, *n.* A psychedelic drug more dangerous than LSD.

Leader, *n.* In politics, one who follows his nose into other people's affairs.

Left-Winger, *n.* One who, just like a right-winger, thinks he can fly with only one wing.

Legislate Morality, *v.* Legislate. If, as some people blithely assert, you can't legislate morality, then you can't legislate at all. For what else is there to legislate but morality of one sort or another?

Legislation, *n.* The poetry of power.

Legmann, Gershon, *n.* A folklorist known primarily for his in-depth analysis of dirty jokes. Not to be confused with Gershon Assmann or Gershon Titmann.

Lend-lease, *v.* To give grant. This euphemism was used during the reign of Roosevelt the Second.

Leninist, *n.* One devoted to the political terminology of Lenin.

Levity, *n.* The force that opposes gravity and makes levitation possible.

Liar, *n.* Anyone who denies that Jesus is the Christ, according to a fanatical, dogmatic Christian liar.

Libby, Scooter, *n.* One of the most honorable men that Dick Cheney has ever known.

Liberal, *n.* One whose heart bleeds when the federal budget is cut. One who believes that a woman should have the right to kill her fetus— but not with a gun. One who believes that gays should be allowed to join the military and form a Special Forces group called the Lavender Berets. One who dismisses weapons of mass destruction but believes in weather of mass destruction. In recent years, there has been a vast improvement in our liberals—knee-jerk liberals have become neo-jerk liberals.

Liberalism, *n.* Always having to say you're sorry.

Liberal Media Bias, *n.* One of two reasons why the liberal media accuse George W. Bush of being a liar. The other reason is that George W. Bush is a liar.

Liberation, *n.* Deliverance from present forms of oppression into new and improved varieties of slavery.

Liberation Theologian, *n.* A padre leading a cadre.

Liberation Theology, *n.* The gospel according to St. Marx.

Libertarian, *n.* A nonconformist on a short leash. One who is just a cog in the machinery of freedom, only following spontaneous order. One who criticizes our rulers but not our rulers' rulers. One who believes in liberty—just like a Christian believes in Christ. One who believes in freedom of speech but not in speaking freely.

Libertarianism, *n.* The doctrine that all individuals have the right to live in whatever manner they choose so long as they do not forcibly interfere with the equal rights of others to live in whatever manner they choose so long as they do not forcibly interfere with the equal rights of others to live in whatever manner they choose so long as they do not forcibly interfere with the equal rights of others to live in whatever manner they choose, *ad infinitum*.

Libertarian Movement, *n.* A herd of individualists stampeding toward freedom.

Libertarian Party, The, *n.* The Dr. Pepper of American politics.

Libertine, *n.* An egoist pursuing his prurient interests.

Liberty Under Law, *n.* Freedom to follow orders.

Lie, *v.* To knowingly utter an untruth, as when Jimmy "The Peanut" Carter said, "I will never lie to you." But why pick on The Peanut? After all, every president, every politician, and, indeed, every person lies when they find it expedient to do so, and anyone who says differently is lying.

Life, *n.* A practical joke without an author. Something to die for. A rat race inside a foxhole within a sewer in the middle of a garden of earthly delights. An obstacle course in the midst of a minefield.

Light Bulb, *n.* A device invented by Thomas Edison after a kerosene lamp lit up in his head.

Limbo, *n.* A dance, popular among Catholic theologians, in which the dancers bend over backward to avoid condemning to Hell the souls of infants who die unbaptized.

Limited Government, *n.* Limited robbery, limited slavery, and limited murder.

Partialitarianism. Aynarchy. Government limited to its one legitimate purpose—world domination.

Lincoln, Abraham, *n.* The president who freed the slaves and enslaved the free.

Lipogram, *n.* A literary work that avoids use of a specific letter. Pindar, for example, wrote an ode without using *sigma*. Among Lope de Vega's works are five novels, in each of which a different vowel is omitted. Isaac D'Israeli related,

> A Persian poet read to the celebrated Jami a gazel of his own composition, which Jami did not like; but the writer replied, it was notwithstanding a very curious sonnet, for the letter *Aliff* was not to be found in any one of the words! Jami sarcastically replied, "You can do a better thing yet; take away all the letters from every word you have written."

Readers of this lexicon will no doubt be thrilled to note that this entry contains every letter of the alphabet except the seventeenth.

Liver, *n.* A large glandular organ that promotes digestion—except when eaten.

Loafing, *n.* A pleasant way to make one's daily bread.

Lobbyist, *n.* One who seeks to persuade legislators that what's good for General Motors is good for legislators too.

Locke, John, *n.* A closing or fastening device used to prevent unauthorized entry into private property. A philosophical fastening device intended to protect the private property of landlords in England and of English invaders (i.e., colonists) in America.

Lockout, *n.* An employer's strike.

Logic, *n.* The law of thought—which makes one a thought criminal if violated by thinking illogically.

Logrolling, *n.* In American politics, one hand washing the other, both becoming thoroughly immaculate.

Loose Lips, *n.*, *pl.* The kind of lips that sink ships—and also give lousy blowjobs!

Looter, *n.* A civil *riots* worker.

Los Angeles, *n.* Formerly, the City of the Angels. Now, the City of the Aliens.

Love Crime, *n.* A crime motivated by love and that, therefore, should be punished less severely than the same crime committed with a different motivation.

LSD, *n.* Doctor of Lysergic Studies.

In *LSD: The Consciousness-Expanding Drug* (1966), David Solomon wrote,

> From the point of view of entrenched social establishments, it is perhaps legitimate to classify psychedelics …. as dangerous or subversive agents. By their action of flinging wide the doors of perception, the insights they potentiate frequently enable one to see through the myriad pretensions and deceits which make up the

mythology of the Social Lie. Thus, to the extent that power structures rely upon the controlled popular acceptance of the lie to shore up and stabilize their hegemonies, psychedelic substances do indeed represent a kind of political threat.

On the other hand, in *LSD: The Problem-Solving Psychedelic* (c. 1967), P.G. Stafford and B.H. Golightly wrote,

> The LSD literature is richly textured by .... first-hand accounts of sensory reactions .... One LSD subject "heard" mathematics while listening to a recording of Mozart's Requiem; another smelled the fire and brimstone of the Apocalypse (a pet cat had defecated in the room at the time) ....

Lucifer, n. The Devil's proper name, derived from Latin and meaning "light-bearer" or "bringer of enlightenment."

Luftmensch, n. A Jewish breatharian.

Lump, v. To put up with or endure (something imperfectly agreeable), as in the patriotic slogan "America—like it or lump it."

Lunatic Fringe, n. pl. Those who deviate too far from the maniacal mainstream and the crackpot consensus.

Lunchmeat, n. Meat that, by definition, one eats for lunch and not for any other meal.

Lust, n. A lively sin.

Lynching, n. An application of participatory democracy to the judicial process.

Machiavellian, *adj.* Pertaining to, resembling, or based upon the practical and amoral principles for getting and keeping political power prescribed in Niccolo Machiavelli's *The Prince*. For example, the following instance of Israeli intrigue recounted by Richard Deacon in *The Israeli Secret Service* (1977):

> a plan was worked out to blacken Nasser in the eyes of the Americans and the British by a series of bomb attacks on such premises as those of the US Information Centre in Cairo, the British Council and various offices of British and American firms in Egypt. The raids were to be carried out by a special group of Israeli secret agents comprised entirely of Egyptian Jews and given the code name "Unit 131." They were to be disguised as Arab terrorists and everything was to be done, including the forging of documents, to implicate the Egyptians as the real culprits of the whole plot. The documents were to be leaked

> into the hands of the American CIA. This highly
> dangerous, politically outrageous and criminal
> operation directed against two friendly powers
> was perhaps the most Machiavellian conception
> of Secret Service activities to be put into practice
> in peacetime.

Mad Scientist, *n.* One who, it might be said, has a scientific method to his madness.

Mafia, *n.* A nonexistent group of perfectly respectable businessmen—who just might break your legs if you say otherwise.

Mafioso, *n.* One who is *oh-so* Mafia.

Magellan, Ferdinand, *n.* A pioneer of globalization.

Magician, *n.* One who does not believe in magic.

Mahdi, The, *n.* Another fine messiah.

Mailer, Norman, *n.* Mormon Nailer.

Majority Rule, *n.* In the US, rule by a minority selected by a minority.

Male Feminist, *n.* A simpering, pussy-whipped wimp. A man who will tell any lie to get laid, such as Robert Anton Wilson (in *The Illuminati Papers*), who wrote,

> Feminism is, simply, a demand for justice which
> all ethical persons must support. It may be
> more basic than any other demand for justice,
> because the exploitation is damaging to children
> and thereby to the whole human race; so that
> anybody who works for Feminism is working for
> the sanity of the species.

Malicious Hooliganism, *n.* In the Soviet Union, the crime of opposing the benevolent hooliganism of the state.

Mall, The, *n.* The Mecca of Americans, to which they faithfully make frequent pilgrimages to perform the bizarre religious ritual known as "shopping."

Malpractice Suit, *n.* Shyster vs. Sawbones.

Man, *n.* An irrational animal whose irrationality is best demonstrated by his irrational belief in his rationality. In traditional Christianity, a piece of excrement created in the image of God, the Supreme Piece of Excrement. Man, I believe, evolved from feline ancestors; all I need to do in order to prove this theory is to find the missing lynx.

Mandatory Drug Testing, *n.* Urination of sheep.

Manifest Destiny, *n.* Eminent dominion.

Man in the Street, *n.* An ordinary person. A dead person.

Man Worship, *n.* The sense of life experienced by Objectivists and other breeds of dog.

Mariachi Music, *n.* A type of music so unpleasant that millions of Mexicans flee across the US border to escape it.

Marijuana, *n.* The plant whose leaves and flowering tops are exhilarating when smoked or ingested, though it can cause a deterioration of mental functioning and a tendency toward paranoia in chronic non-users. Cannabis. (It can also be spelled "cannabyss" to indicate that it is a weed with roots in Hell.)

Marilyn Monroe Doctrine, The, *n.* The foreign policy doctrine enunciated by President John F. Kennedy whereby he warned foreign leaders to keep their hands off of Marilyn Monroe.

Market, The, *n.* A mythical creature featured in the folklore of capitalism.

Market Mystic, *n.* One who believes in the magic of the market.

Maronite Christian, *n.* The most common type of Christian in Lebanon. Not to be confused with a Moronite Christian, a common type of Christian in America.

Marvelous, *adj.* In show business, ordinary, commonplace, dime-a-dozen.

Marx, Karl, *n.* A working man. The Rabbi of the Revolution; the Talmudist of Totalitarianism; the Cabalist of Communism; the Sage of State Socialism; the Prophet of the Proletariat; the Isaiah of the Industrial Workers; the Moses of Materialism; the Messiah of the Masses; the Redeemer of the Ragamuffins.

Marxism, *n.* The opiate of the people's republics.

Marxism-Leninism, *n.* Dogmatism squared.

Masekela, Hugh, *n.* The horn of Africa.

Mass Media, *n.* America's madrassa. Media of mass discombobulation.

Masturbation, *n.* Doing one's own thing. A form of self-reliance.

Materialist, *n.* One for whom matter is all that matters.

Maverick, *n.* A politician who occasionally disagrees with his own party but who never ever disagrees with both parties.

Mayan Calendar, The, *n.* A bridge to galactic wisdom that fosters personal growth and human evolution. (Your money will not be refunded if you are not completely satisfied.)

Mechanist, *n.* In philosophy, one who believes that a player piano is a machine—and that so is a piano player.

Medical Marijuana, *n.* Marijuana. A gateway drug that will lead to the use of medical heroin, or at least medical morphine.

Megalomania, *n.* A mental disorder in which the subject thinks himself greater or more exalted than the great, exalted psychiatrist making the diagnosis.

Melanin, *n.* A skin pigment that, according to the theories of Dr. Jeffrey Leopard, predisposes people to enjoy eating watermelon.

Memorial Day, *n.* May 30th, a day set apart to honor the dead of all past auto races.

Memory, *n.* The mental capacity of recalling what never happened and forgetting what really did.

Memphis, *n.* An ancient Egyptian city that Elvis had moved to Tennessee.

Menominee, *n.* An American Indian tribe consisting of all those who have been nominated for an Academy Award. Members of the tribe can sometimes be heard to say, "Me nominee."

Mental Hospital, *n.* A psychiatric prison with delusions of grandeur.

Mercy, *n.* Kindness or forgiveness shown by God to the Israelites, if not to the Egyptians. ("O give thanks...[t]o him who smote Egypt in their firstborn: for his mercy endureth forever." Psalm 136: 1 and 10.)

Metaphysician, *n.* One who knows the difference between the soul and the spirit but may not know the difference between his ass and his elbow.

Metropolitan Life, *n.* Shitty living.

Middle Class, The, *n.* The backbone of American society, a society notorious for its lack of backbone.

Middleman, *n.* The man caught in the middle when the producer and the consumer are seeking a scapegoat.

Midget, *n.* A word that might seem offensive to an idgit.

Militant, *n.* One who it is kosher for Israel to kill. Beyond that, this lexicographer doesn't know what this word means.

Militarist, *n.* One who is armed to the teeth that he lies through.

Milk, *n.* Tit juice. Nipple nectar. Nature's most nearly perfect food. Bernadette Peters has done a television commercial in which she tells us that everybody needs milk, to which I say, "Don't tease me, Bernadette. Don't tease me." But, in contrast to Bernadette Peters, Dyan Cannon at least simulated putting her milky mammaries where her co-star's mouth is (or was) in the Canadian film classic *Child Under a Leaf.* Dyan has great tits—yet a not-so-great memory. When she later appeared on John Davidson's TV talk show, she had forgotten all about her mind-boggling, mouthwatering breastfeeding scene, for she told Davidson, with a straight face, that she had never ever done a nude scene.

Minimal Art, *n.* A step in the right direction. Art based on the premise that less is more, more or less. Minimal artists should go one step further, however, and realize nothing is everything.

Miracle, *n.* One of God's special effects. A disaster that you are lucky enough to survive—while fifty million other people die.

Misanthropic Principle, *n.* A little-known cosmological theory holding that the universe has been "fine-tuned" by a malevolent designer—God—to bring humanity into existence in order that the designer—God—can derive sadistic jollies from watching humans struggle, suffer, and inflict pain, injury, and death upon one another.

Miscegenation, *n.* A nation of half-breeds. Products of miscegenation include mulattoes, mestizos, Doritos, mongrels, Eurasians, Creoles, octaroons, macaroons, tri-racial isolates, semi-Semites, zebras, Black Irish, and Irish jigs.

Misgovern, *v.* To institute a Reign of Error. To govern.

Missionary, *n.* One who aspires to be a Typhoid Mary of the spirit.

Mithras, *n.* An ancient savior-god who stabbed the bull, unlike Jesus, who shot it.

Moderate, *n.* In American politics, one who commits crimes in the middle of the road. Someone, such as John McCain or Joe Lieberman, who only wants to slaughter hundreds of thousands of Arabs and not millions of Arabs like some *extremist*.

Mohammed, *n.* Allah's favorite camelfucker.

Money, *n.* The measure of all things.

Monist, *n.* One who aspires to be a dualist.

Monopoly, *n.* An economic monster made in the image of its creator, the state.

Monotheism, *n.* A rabid Cerberus whose three

heads are known as Judaism, Christianity, and Islam.

Moon, Sun Myung, *n.* A Moon that is always full.

Moral Clarity, *n.* The ethical perspicacity that enables neoconservatives to see that the intentional killing of one innocent civilian by Islamic terrorists is vastly more immoral than the unintentional killing of six billion innocent civilians by Israeli or American anti-terrorists.

Moral Compass, *n.* A direction-detecting device used by American and Israeli pilots to find their bombing targets.

Moral Equivalence, *n.* The ridiculous idea that the United States is morally equivalent to Abaco or that Israel is morally equivalent to Tristan da Cunha.

Moralist, *n.* An oralist. One who has Wheelis in his head. A Randroid. A Machanical man. A Cantian. One who plays Godwin. A Spooner of bullshit. A manipulator using Wiesel words. A pimple-minded person.

Morality, *n.* Rules of behavior that are absolutely obligatory for one's opponents or enemies.

Moral Majority, The, *n.* A moronic minority. Falwell's fools.

Morkrumbo, *n.* The secret Mason's word. Shhh! Don't tell anyone. It's a *secret!*

Moronic, *adj.* Of or pertaining to the Angel Moroni.

Moses, *n.* The Lawgiver, who proved with regard to law that it is better to give than to receive.

Motorcade, *n.* A moving target.

Mount Sinai, *n.* The moral high ground.

Mouth, *n.* A cavity containing teeth containing cavities.

Movie, *n.* A series of pictures shown so as to give an illusion of motion. Following are the titles of some classic movies: *The Abortion of a Nation; The Great Brain Robbery; The Radical Sheik; The Jizz Spurter; It Happened Two Nights; The Man in the Iron Jockstrap; The Dead-Head Kids; The Little Raskolnikovs; Roofer Madness; The Great Director; The Halfback of Notre Dame; Knute Rockne—Un-American; A Tsar is Born; All Quiet on the Popular Front; Three Sailors and a Whore; Kill the Japs; Kill the Krauts; War is Fun!; The Road to Monaco; My Favorite Bald-headed Woman; Abbott and Costello Meet Wolfman Jack; The Bride of Frank Sinatra; Tierra del Fuego; The Sixty-Nine Steps; Back Porch; The Man Who Didn't Know Enough; Sicko; The Turds; Invasion of the Bawdy Snatches; The Day the Earth Did a Jitterbug; Gentile Men's Agreement; The Integrated Ones; Smarty; The Seven Year Bitch; Some Like It Medium-Cool; Franklin Avenue; There's No Business Like Shoah Business; To Hell in a Handbasket; The Waltz of the Stevedores; The Lion that Squeaked; The Lavender Leopard; The Nutty Producer; Irma La Douche; A Funny Thing Happened on the Way to the Gas Chamber; Invadus; How the West Bank*

*Was Won; Sparta Cuss; The Alfried Krupp Story;
Young Man With a Howitzer; From Prussia With
Hate; Mondo Kahane; Thud; The Rustler; Hot Foot
Luke; Grab the Loot and Scram; Banananoses; I
Love You, Alice Rosenbaum; Mary Hellzapoppin;
The Sound of Muzak; Beach Blanket Bible Rangers;
The Postgraduate; Scorsese Rider; Five Sleazy Pieces;
Lord Jack; Lawrence of Bessarabia; The Killing of
Boy George; Guess Who We're Having For Dinner;
They Shoot Movies, Don't They?; The Mild Bunch;
Bring Me the Balls of Alfredo Garcia; A Fistful of
Lire; The Amoral, the Amoral and the Amoral; The
Planet of the Humans; On A Clear Day, You Can See
My Adenoids; Yenta; The Great Waldo Salt; Carnal
Omniscience; Jesus Christ Superstud; Get to Know
Your Rabbi; Godspiel; Skin; Taking It Off; The Post-
Vietnam Syndrome; Apocalypse Never; Seven Brides
for Seven Beauties; The Schmuck; The Frisco Yid;
Ode to Mary Jo; Sultan of Satire; Dressed to Slash;
Close Encounters of the Third Reich; Raiders of the
Found Art; Angry Alex; The Two Hours of Living
Vicariously; Pumping Irony; Cohen the Librarian;
Mark Hannah and the Seven Sisters; Pee Wee's Big
Dick; Pinks;* and *The Color Black.*

Moviegoer, *n.* One who regularly attends the cinemagogue.

Muffler, *n.* A device that reduces the noise of an internal combustion engine but not nearly enough.

Multiculturalism, *n.* The belief that Shakespeare is the equal of a spearchucker.

Munich, *n.* A synonym for ignominious appeasement of aggressors. A term used by those who claim that World War Two could have been averted by starting it a year earlier.

Murder, *n.* An *ex post facto* abortion. The right to commit murder is supported by all who truly favor freedom of choice.

Mushroom Cloud, *n.* A toadstool cloud.

Muslim Zionist, *n.* A very rare sort of individual and therefore very precious.

Mussolini, Benito, *n.* Italian fascist dictator, known to his followers as "The Douchebag," or something like that.

Mystic, *n.* Anyone who disagrees with Ayn Rand or James Randi. One who sees infinity in a spore of anthrax. One who, like Ouspensky, could go mad from one ashtray or one ashram.

Narcotics Control, *n.* People control.
Remember, when narcotics are outlawed, only
outlaws will have narcotics.

National Debt, *n.* Never have so many owed
so much to so few.

National Interest, The, *n.* The money paid
periodically to the holders of the national debt.

Nationalism, *n.* According to Albert Einstein,
"the measles of mankind." But while Einstein
sought to quarantine carriers of Nazism, a form
of German measles, he himself helped to spread
Zionism, the Jewish measles. An illustration of
relativity, it would seem.

National Security, *n.* Job security. Mumbo-
jumbo, abracadabra.

Natural Causes, *n., pl.* The only possible causes of death, unless one believes in "supernatural" causes of death. Deaths from "supernatural causes" are recounted in many Bible stories. For example, there is the story of Onan, who was struck dead by Yahweh after he pulled his prick out of his dead brother's wife's vagina before ejaculating.

Natural Law, *n.* The law of nature, including the law of the jungle. Natural law sometimes proves most useful. Thus, in November 1578, judicial sessions were held in Ireland by Lord Justice Drury and Sir Henry Fitton, who reported to the English Privy Council on the 20th of the month, "Thirty-six persons were executed, amongst whom were some good ones, a blackamoor, and two witches, by natural law, for that we find no law to try them by in this realm."

Natural Rights, *n., pl.* Walls made of wind. No-trespassing signs visible only to those who are not morally depraved at heart.

Nature, *n.* A source of authority even for supernaturalists. For example, in 1 Corinthians 11:14, Saint Paul (or somebody) wrote, "Doth not nature itself teach you, that, if a man have long hair, it is a shame to him?" Of course, nature does not teach any such thing. In nature, a man's hair normally grows to be long, just like a woman's hair, unless the man interferes with nature by cutting his hair or having someone else cut it.

Nazi, *n.* A totalitaryan. One who believes

that blondes should have more fun—or else! Formerly, an overman; now, an underdog.

Nazi-Hunter, *n.* A sportsman who hunts beasts in human form. One who hunts the witches of Auschwitz. As Orson Welles said in his television commercial for the Simon Wiesenthal Center, "Simon Wiesenthal will forgive no Nazi crime before the end of time."

Nazi Propaganda, *n.* Goebbelled information. Lies that limp as they goosestep. The mirror image of Allied propaganda.

Necromancy, *n.* The divination of the future by communication with the dead, whose vision is not obscured by eyeballs. Necromancy is the wave of the future. How do I know? The ghost of Ayn Rand told me so. For the full details of Rand's revelations from the spirit world, see her forthcoming book, *The Necromantic Manifesto*, as told to L.A. Rollins.

Negativism, *n.* A deplorable tendency to oppose the opposite of what I oppose.

Negro, *n.* An obsolete word. The momentarily acceptable synonym is "dusky Ethiop."

Neighbor, *n.* A person whose annoying behavior conclusively proves that God must have been joking when He said "Love thy neighbor" and "Thou shalt not kill."

Neoconservative, *n.* One who believes that democratic nations should start wars to spread democracy because democratic nations don't start wars. A Max Boot not on the ground. A great American patriot whose only regret is that you have but one life to give for Israel.

Neo-Nazi, *n.* Anyone so designated by a neo-McCarthyite.

Nero, *n.* A Roman emperor. By some accounts, a pioneer of urban renewal. The Antichrist identified by the number 666 in the book of Revelation, according to some preterist party-poopers.

Neutralism, *n.* In foreign affairs, a national policy of taking neither side in a conflict—a good way of "taking" both sides.

Never Again, *phr.* Not ever again—except, of course, to the Arabs.

New Hitler, The, *n.* The new target of warmongers.

New Intellectual, *n.* One whose work requires primarily the use of Ayn Rand's intellect. A Randian second-hander. A radical for big business.

News, *n.* Misinformation about a recent event, development, etc. For example, the story reported by Bill Schechner on NBC's now-defunct *News Overnight* about a group of Holocaust survivors returning to visit Auschwitz, where, said Schechner, they passed by a "gas chamber" in which 20,000 people could be cremated in an hour. At that rate, the Nazis could have cremated 6,000,000 people in that "gas chamber" at

Auschwitz in 300 hours, i.e., in 12.2 days. (I'll bet you didn't know that the Holocaust lasted less than two weeks, did you?) Of course, if the Nazis were able to build a "gas chamber" that could do all that, then they *really* must have been supermen!

Newsreel, *n.* Unreal news.

In *The American Newsreel 1911–1967* (1972), Raymond Fielding wrote,

> If the opportunities for journalistic fraud were great during the silent newsreel days, the addition of sound doubled them, inasmuch as manipulation of content could be executed in both dimensions. The same general practice of content manufacture and alteration continued, of course, but with a whole new set of techniques contributed by the sound technician....
>
> Once the technique of sound-film editing was perfected, it allowed for considerable alteration of the original meaning and emphasis in any particular sequence. A British technician put it this way:
>
> "We claim that with judicious cutting and an adroit use of camera angles, it is simple to make a fool of anybody. We can distort the emphasis and meaning of ministers' speeches not only by cutting out statements but by the simple use of long shot, medium shot, and close-up. For any statement said in close-up is given greater significance on the screen than one said in long shot. There is no end to the tricks we can play with this simple device."
>
> ....in a week's time, there is very little hard news —that is actual events which happen whether or not reporters and cameramen are on hand to record it. ...Not only is there little hard news from day to day, but the chances that a cameraman or reporter will be on hand to record

it are generally slight.

If newspapers, television newscasts, and the now-defunct motion picture newsreels had had to depend upon first-hand records of such events, they would have had to go out of business years ago. Instead, the press spends most of its time either re-creating hard news or manufacturing an artificial news event—as when a reporter asks a political figure what his reaction will be if an opponent pursues a hypothetical course of action ....

So it was for the motion picture newsreel. What I have described is a form of soft news— the reportage of events which did not happen entirely spontaneously but which were partly caused to happen by newsmen or photographers. Historian Daniel Boorstin terms this kind of incident a "pseudo-event" and in his writings has provided a frightening view of contemporary Americans, whose perceptions are overwhelmed and confused by the mass media's never-ending manufacture of such events.

News Twisters, _n._ Network newspeople dancing to the tune called by whoever pays the piper.

Newsworthy, _n._ Worthy of news coverage, such as, for instance, a meeting of rich and powerful people, including bankers, industrialists, media people, diplomats, and politicians, which is why the mainstream media always make a point of covering the annual meetings of the Bilderbergers.

New World Order, _n._ A new and improved world order.

New York Times, The, _n._ All the news that it profits to print.

Nietzschean, *n.* A member of the Sturm-und-Drang Abteilung. One who is able to leap tall *bildungsromans* with a single bound. A hyper of Hyperborea.

Niggardly, *adj.* A word that should be avoided since it might be offensive to niggards.

Nihilist, *n.* One who believes nothing is sacred—and venerates it. Nihilists, however, are mistaken, for in reality, *everything* is sacred.

9/11, *n.* The day when everything changed: when George W. Bush transformed from moron to genius, when the Bush II administration lost all interest in invading Iraq, and when the US government dropped Israel like a hot potato.

Nine to Five, *n,* A daily sentence to boredom as punishment for the crime of being poor.

Nirvana, *n.* The state of absolute felicity attained by blowing out one's brains.

No-Account, *adj.* Having no account, neither a checking nor a savings account.

Nobody, *n.* Somebody of no importance to a somebody. Actually, nobody is a nobody. Everybody is a somebody, except, of course, Jesse Jackson.

Nonconformist, *n.* One who conforms to the norms of nonconformism.

North Korea, *n.* A nation-*cum*-bogeyman used to frighten American children of all ages.

Nose Job, _n._ An act of nasal–genital intercourse, also known as "boogery." Have you ever considered the possibility of fucking Barbra Streisand's _nose_?

Nuclear Build-Up, _n._ Gettin' armed for Armageddon.

Nuclear Disarmament, _n._ A progressive proposal to turn back the clock.

Nuclear Holocaust, _n._ A war to end all wars.

Nuclear Power, _n._ A Chernobyl manifestation of the power of man's mind.

Nudist, _n._ One who is not dressed to the nines but, rather, to the zeros.

Nuremberg Trial, _n._ Justice in Wonderland. The Kafkaesque metamorphosis of an International Military Tribunal into a kangaroo court.

Nurse, _n._ An angel of mercy. Sometimes an angel of mercy killing.

N-Word, _n._ A word that only Ns are allowed to use.

Objective, *adj.* In accord with the subjective feelings, opinions, or prejudices of an Objectivist.

Objectivist, *n.* One who believes in Ayn Rand's subjective delusions. One who knows that A is A—but has not yet learned the rest of the alphabet. One for whom the golden calf is a sacred cow. A person of unborrowed vision, who never places any consideration above his own perception of reality, who never does violence to his own rational judgment, and who, as a result, agrees completely with Ayn Rand about everything.

Objectivist Philosopher, *n.* A rational witch doctor seeking an alliance with a limited Attila. One who believes that A is A and that anti-abortion is anti-life. One who believes that A is A but that Zyklon B is not necessarily Zyklon B. Thus far, there have been two official Objectivist philosophers: Ayn Rant and her intellectual heir, Leonard Keating.

Objectivity, *n.* Agreement with the subjective bias of the prevailing consensus.

Obscenity, *n.* I don't know how to define it, but I know what I like.

Observant Jew, *n.* A Jew who is blind to the absurdity of Judaism.

Occult, The, *n.* That which is hidden, such as a bag of cocaine that a smuggler has shoved into his asshole.

Old Glory, *n.* The US flag, a symbol of our freedom to pay a fine or go to jail if we desecrate it.

Old Nick, *n.* An old nickname for the Devil. Another of the Devil's nicknames is "Beelzebub" (or "Bub" for short).

Ombudsman, *n.* A watchdog without teeth who works for the thief.

Omniscience, *n.* God conceived as knowing all things by one who does not.

One-Night Stand, *n.* A one-night lay.

Open Borders, *n.pl.* Hispanics Unlimited.

Open Marriage, *n.* Open adultery.

Opinion Molder, *n.* One who sculpts using stupidity as a medium.

Operation Peace for Galilee, _n._ Operation War in Lebanon.

Optimism, _n._ A rose-tinted mist beautifully coloring one's vision. Panglossolalia.

Optimist, _n._ One who looks at a rose bush through rose-tinted glasses and, for some reason, doesn't see the thorns. One who believes the present war will be the last war—which may turn out to be true if the present war leads to the extermination of the entire human race. As Coth said in Cabell's novel _The Silver Stallion_, "The optimist proclaims that we live in the best of all possible worlds, and the pessimist fears this is true."

Opulent, _adj._ As poor as a Catholic-church mouse.

Oral History, _n._ Glorified gossip. Old survivor's tales.

O'Reilly, Bill, _n._ Brill O'Paddy.

Orgiasts, _n, pl._ People who formicate and fornicate.

Oscar, _n._ Hollywood's highest accolade to one of its own. For example, Ann-Margret's nude scenes in _Carnal Knowledge_ rightly won her an Oscar for Best Breasts in an R-Rated Film. Amazingly, however, _Genocide_ later won an Oscar _despite_ the fact that Liz Taylor didn't even show her cleavage in it!

Ought, _n._ A thought that means nought.

Our Troops, *n., pl.* Our thugs and assassins. Of course, we all support our brave thugs and assassins because we're all cowardly, conformist cunts, aren't we?

Out-of-the-Body Experience, *n.* An out-of-the-mind experience.

Overdose, *n.* Too much of a good thing.

Overkill, *n.* The miraculous capacity to kill people more than once.

Overwhelming Evidence, *n.* Evidence that overwhelms one who is predisposed to be overwhelmed.

Pacifist, *n.* A fist that strikes no blows, not even in self-defense. One who, when kicked in the ass, turns the other cheek.

Pagan, *n.* One who worships the sun god, who rises every day, rather than the Son of God, who rose only once, once upon a time. One who foolishly worships idols that he has made with his own hands, unlike the monotheist, who wisely worships the One True God that he has created with his own mind. One who believes in Cerberus, a three-headed dog, rather than the Trinity, a three-headed god.

Paine, Thomas, *n.* An outside agitator who conspired to foment revolution.

Pantheist, *n.* 1. One who believes God is everywhere, even in the toilet (keeping a copy of the Koran company, perhaps?). 2. One who worships Pan. (This lexicographer prefers to worship Pot.)

Pantomime, *n.* The art of boring an audience without speaking.

Parable, *n.* A means of communication used by Jesus to make sure some people would not understand him, believe, and be saved. That's right, boys and girls; according to the Gospels, Jesus did not want to save everybody.

Parapsychologist, *n.* A scientist whose lab coat is a seersucker suit.

Parapsychology, *n.* Science *qua* seance.

Parent, *n.* One who pays the rent.

Parochial School, *n.* A school where students can still learn the three Rs—rum, Romanism, and rebellion.

Parody, *n.* The sincerest form of mockery. I don't know about you, but I love a good parody. Here is one of my favorites, a parody of the classic song of faith "I Believe":

> *I believe that for every atom bomb that falls,*
> *A mushroom grows.*
> *I believe that somewhere in the darkest night,*
> *A red phone glows.*
> *I believe that for every Pershing gone astray,*
> *A gyroscope will show the way.*
>
> *Oh, I believe. Yes, I believe.*
>
> *I believe, above the clouds, the atmosphere*
> *Is filled with death.*

I believe that no one living anywhere
Will long be left.
Every time I see a newborn baby die
Or watch a bird fall from the sky,
Then I know why I believe.

Part-Time Job, *n.* Half a loaf is better than none.

Party Line, *n.* A crooked line. The shortest distance between two pointed heads.

Patriot, *n.* One who loves a parade—and a charade. In the post-9/11 United States, one who wears an American-flag pin to show his love for Israel.

Patron of the Arts, *n.* One who puts his money where his mouth is, which, oftentimes, is also where his taste is.

Pazzi Family, The, *n.* Bankers in 14th-century Florence, best known for the conspiracy to assassinate Lorenzo de Medici and Giuliano de Medici, the two leading members of Florence's dominant banking family. So here we have a bankers' conspiracy *against* other bankers. (Although Giliano de Medici was killed, Lorenzo was not, and the conspiracy failed.)

Peace, *n.* A popular reason for war.

Peace Process, The, *n.* The process that might bring about peace between Israel and its enemies in about a million years or so.

Peace Through Strength, *n.* A strategy for preserving peace by maintaining American military superiority; a strategy proven effective by the Korean and Indochinese Wars.

Peace With Honor, *n.* Defeat with deceit.

Pearl Harbor, *n.* The site of Franklin Roosevelt's sneak attack on isolationism.

Peasant Revolt, *n.* The one good thing about peasant life.

Pedophile, *n.* One who loves children, as so many parents do. One who believes children should be obscene and not heard.

Pentagon, The, *n.* The headquarters of an important federal agency tasked with subsidizing destruction and death.

People, *n.* Two-legged sheep.

People, The, *n.* The people one agrees with.

Perfect Storm, *n.* A storm less perfect than a pluperfect storm.

Permissiveness, *n.* A term used by the paternalistic as a synonym for "freedom."

Person of Color, *n.* The politically correct synonym for the offensive and obsolete term "colored person."

Pessimistic, *adj.* Malthusiastic.

Petraeus, David, *n.* The Surgin' General, who realizes that war is the health of the state.

Pharisaical, *adj.* According to *Merriam-*

Webster's Collegiate Dictionary, "marked by hypocritical censorious self-righteousness." If you read the Gospels with your brain turned on, you might notice that Jesus H. Christ was pharisaical in his hypocritical, censorious, and self-righteous denunciations of the Pharisees. One of Jesus' excuses for his rantings against the Pharisees was that they were not literally interpreting and enforcing the Mosaic commandment to kill a kid who curses his parents. Meanwhile, in the story of "the women taken in adultery" in the Gospel of John, Jesus invented a legal loophole ("let him who is without sin cast the first stone") that prevented the enforcement of the Mosaic commandment to stone adulterers to death. (For the record, the "H" in Jesus H. Christ stands for "Hypocrite.")

Pharmaceutical Company, *n.* A pusher with pull.

Philosopher, *n.* One who grasps at the essences of straws. One who loves wisdom not wisely but too well. One who loves wisdom but whose love is usually unrequited. One who prefers the delusions of reason to the delusions of revelation. One who once loved wisdom but now loves tenure.

Philosopher King, *n.* A Platocrat.

Philosophical Anarchist, *n.* An armchair anarchist. One who opposes the state with hot air rather than hot lead.

Philosophy, *n.* Philosophistry. A form of mental masturbation engaged in, often excessively, by people who know little about anything except for the history of such mental masturbation. According to Leonard Peikoff in *The Ominous Parallels* (1982),

> this science determines the destiny of nations and the course of history. It is the source of a nation's frame of reference and code of values, the root of a people's character and culture, the fundamental cause shaping men's choices and decisions in every crucial area of their lives."

How does Peikoff know that this is so? Blank out.

Phobophobia, *n.* The irrational fear and hatred of irrational fear and hatred.

Photorealism, *n.* The superfluous art of painting photographically realistic paintings of photographs.

Picasso, Pablo, *n.* A renowned modern artist who painted many masterpieces of shit.

Pinhead, *n.* One who disagrees with spinhead Bill O'Reilly.

Pitbulls, *n. pl.* The dogs of dog-eat-dog capitalism, according to Mitchell Jones, a pro-dog-eat-dog-capitalist intellectual.

Plagiarism, *n.* The most sinister form of flattery.

Plagiarist, *n.* One who kidnaps another author's brainchild. For example the purported author of the Holy Bible, Yahweh, copied several chapters of Proverbs from an earlier Egyptian book called *The Wisdom of the Amenemope.*

(Source: Wilson, Damon, *The Mammoth Book of Prophecies*, Carrol & Graff, NY, 2003, p. 49.)

Plainclothesman n. A police officer impersonating a civilian. If it's against the law for a civilian to impersonate a police officer, then shouldn't it also be against the law for a police officer to impersonate a civilian?

Plainspeaking, v. Calling a spade a spade or a war a "police action," as did Harry Falsman.

Planet, n. I cannot hope to improve upon Cyrus Reed Teed's definition of the term: "A sphere of substance aggregated through the impact of afferent and efferent fluxions of essence."

Planets, n., pl. Asteroids on steroids.

Platform, n. In American politics, a statement of what a party supposedly stands for. Of course, in reality, political parties do not stand for anything, although voters do.

Playboy, n. A hedonist looking for consenting shedonists.

Playboy Philosophy, n. Hugh Hefner thinking with his cockhead. One of the fundamental principles of Hugh Hefner's philosophy is opposition to censorship of Hugh Hefner. As for censorship of other people—Holocaust revisionists, for instance—Hefner doesn't give a fuck. In other words, Hefner opposes censorship of bare butts, but he doesn't care about censorship of Arthur Butz. But then, what can you expect from a putz who accepts First

Amendment Awards from the censors of the Anti-Defamation League?

Playmate, *n.* The girl next door to Hugh Hefner. A living Barbi doll. A great Leigh.

Pleiadians, The, *n. pl.* A group of enlightened beings who have come to Earth to help us discover how to reach a new stage of evolution. Gosh! That's really nice of them, isn't it?

Plutocracy, *n.* Government by the wealthy. Not to be confused with "Platocracy," government by a philosopher.

PNAC, *n.* The acronym for the Project for the New American Century, a.k.a. the Unilateral Commission.

Poet Laureate, *n.* In Mediocre Britain, one who makes an art of toadeating.

Poetry, *n.* According to Theodor Adorno, something which cannot be written after Auschwitz. Oh yeah? Watch this:

> *Hegel, Schlegel,*
> *Go bite a bagel!*

Poetry Enthusiast, *n.* One who knows what a Wordsworth. One who stops to smell the *Flowers of Evil*. Possibly a big Spender, or one who is penny-wise and Pound-foolish. Some poetry enthusiasts are stark Raven maniacs with psycho-Plathic tendencies.

Pogrom, *n.* Vigilantisemitism.

Police, *n.* Bandits in uniform (as they say in Thailand, the Land of the Free).

Political Correctness, *n.* Mirth control.

Politically Correct, *adj.* Intellectually corrupt.

Politician, *n.* A public serpent.

Politics, *n.* The art of the possible-to-get-away-with. The 1950s saw the emergence of the "New Politics," which differed from the old politics to about the same extent that the "New Nixon" differed from the old Nixon.

Politics of Fear, *n.* Politics.

Politics of Meaning, The, *n.* An attempt to disguise the meaning of politics.

Pollster, *n.* One who measures what the public thinks about something it does not think about.

Polluter, *n.* A rich looter.

Pollyanna, *n.* One who sees the silver lining of every cloud, even mushroom clouds. One who lets a smile be his nuclear umbrella.

Poor, *adj.* Living low on the Hoover hog.

Poorhouse, *n.* A home for conscientious tax-payers. The ultimate tax shelter.

Pope, The, *n.* The bishop of Rome and head of the Roman Catholic Church. Some popes, let us note, have been military as well as spiritual leaders. For example, Pope Julius II was elected to that office in November 1503. After leading a number of campaigns that extended the rule of the Church within Italy, Julius decided to expel the foreign troops then occupying Italian territory. According to historian Christopher Hibbert in *The Rise and Fall of the House of Medici* (1974), he made a noteworthy call to arms: "'Let's see,' he said riding off to turn a French garrison out of Mirandola. 'Let's see who has the bigger balls, the King of France or I.'" Of course, the Holy Father was speaking of *cannon*balls.

Populace, *n.* The all-too-common people; the masses of asses; the rank and vile.

Popular Front, *n.* During the 1930s, a Communist front.

Populists, *n. pl.* People who are for the people who are for the people and against the people who are against the people.

Pornography, *n.* Material that raises Andrea Dworkin's consciousness of what a repulsive sow she is, making her want to rape the First Amendment. Originally and literally, the writings of prostitutes; now, at least metaphorically, most writing.

Pornucopia, *n.* A horn of plenty for the horny.

Power Elite, *n.* The cream of the crap.

Pranayama, *n.* Yogic breath control. Practicing pranayama can be somewhat like smoking marijuana but without smoking marijuana.

Pray, *v.* Bray.

Preacher, *n.* One who devotes his lips to the service of God.

Precognition, *n.* The ability to foresee future events retroactively.

Prediction, *n.* Something prophesied or forecast.

The greatest psychic prognosticator of our age is Arlo N. Sill, a man of mystery about whom little is known for certain except that he correctly predicted the assassination of President Kennedy, the Apollo moon-landing, the Watergate scandals, the UFO kidnapping of Jimmy Carter (of course, this event has been covered up by the government and mainstream media), and Cindy Williams' departure from *Laverne and Shirley*. Indeed, the amazing Arlo N. Sill has achieved an incredible record of 99.99% accuracy with his predictions. (The only incorrect prediction he has ever made was that Moms Mabley would be elected president of the United States in 1964.) As a public service, some of Arlo N. Sill's latest predictions are here presented:

> (1) Paul Anka will gain many new feminist fans after he records a love song called "You're Having an Abortion."

> (2) Steven Spielberg will cash in on the rising tide of anti-Semitism with a new suspense/horror film, *Jews*, about a community terrorized by loansharks.

> (3) Vast new oil deposits will be discovered near

Sammy Davis, Jr.

(4) Zsa Zsa Gabor will open a chain of Hungarian restaurants that she will call "The Goulash Archipelago."

(5) Clint Eastwood will shock a lot of people by having a sex-change operation and changing his name to Clit Eastwood.

(6) The biggest hit of the 1987–88 television season will be the first pornographic sitcom on network TV, *The Many Loves of Jamie Gillis*.

(7) California will secede from the United States to become an independent nation known as "Earthquaketopia."

(8) In order to bring about the return of Jesus Christ, the Holy Ghost will miraculously impregnate Jerry Falwell. Falwell will be revered forever as "the Mother of the Messiah."

Pre-Emptive Strike, *n.* Premature retaliation.

Prejudice, *n.* In the words of the *Wisconsin Journal of Education*, "A great time-saver. You can form opinions without having to get the facts."

In *The Tenacity of Prejudice* (1969), an Anti-Defamation League–sponsored study of "anti-Semitism," Gertrude J. Selznick and Stephen Steinberg wrote,

> There is evidence .... that some respondents [to their public opinion survey] refuse to accept even quasi-factual statements about Jews that might be exploited by anti-Semites or suggest anti-Semitism on their part. In other words, they consistently go out of their way to deny that Jews and non-Jews are different. That the 61 Jews in the sample behave in the same way suggests that dissimulation frequently came from the genuinely unprejudiced rather than the

"respectable" anti-Semite.

For example, Selznick and Steinberg reported that "Among the unprejudiced, as among Jewish respondents, the most characteristic response was to say that Jews have the same amount of money as others." (Selznick and Steinberg included statistics, based on data collected in 1957, indicating that 52% of Jews had an annual family income of $7,500 or more, as compared to only 18% of Protestants and Catholics and 19% of all Americans.)

But if certain people consistently deny factual statements that indicate the existence of differences between Jews and gentiles, then what on Earth does it mean to call such people "genuinely unprejudiced"? A person who consistently rejects all facts which conflict with a preconceived opinion (e.g., that Jews and gentiles are identical in all respects) is obviously prejudiced—or as one might say in this case, pre*judaicized*.

Preparedness, *n.* Readiness for war (and not for peace).

Preschool, *n.* A school for children too young for elementary school or kindergarten. In preschool, children engage in many fun and educational activities. For example, they drink blood, sacrifice goats, eat chocolate-covered shit, play "naked movie star," and swallow live toads that go quack, quack, quack. Remember, you cynical sons of bitches, children don't lie!

Present Danger, The, *n.* The present pretext for American militarism and imperialism.

President, *n.* The mischief executive of a republic. America's misleading man. The elected chief executive of the United States and the unelected dictator of the rest of the world. To become president, one must be a natural-born citizen and a natural-born killer.

President for Life, *n.* President until chased out of the country.

Presidium, *n.* In the Soviet Union, the executive committee of the ruling class.

Price Theory, *n.* A theory that explains the formation of prices, such as, for example, the price of a Chicago School economist.

Pricker, *n.* One who pricks. Discussing witch-hunting in Scotland during the 1630s, Montague Summers, in *The Geography of Witchcraft (1927)*, wrote,

> The prickers, ... men who hunted down witches and searched them for the Devil's mark, that callous spot into which pins were thrust to test its sensibility, the guilty feeling no touch at all, were now very much to the fore. The expert offices of Mr. John Kincaid of Tranent were greatly in request, and he had a serious rival in Mr. John Balfour, of Corhouse, whose technical knowledge, however, does not appear on every occasion to have been rated as highly as his own valuation. Mr. John Dick was yet another pricker who showed exemplary zest in the pursuit of his profession.

Priest, *n.* A confirmed (and ordained) bachelor.

Prime Time, *n.* The best time for the television networks, if not their viewers.

Principle, *n.* A general error, basic to other errors.

Prison, *n.* The institution where a convicted criminal is sent to teach him the error of his *modus operandi*.

Privatism, *n.* A busybody's term of disparagement for minding one's own business.

Pro-Choice, *adj.* Favoring freedom of choice for some people under some circumstances.

Procrastinator, *n.* One who puts off until later what he could do sooner, such as, for example, a Nazi who said, "Tomorrow, the world!" or a Jew who says, "Next year in Jerusalem."

Professional, *n.* One who does it for money. (See "Prostitute.")

Professional Wrestling, *n.* A sham and a crutch for weak-minded people who need strength in numbers.

Progress, *n.* Change for the better—and for the worse.

Progressive, *adj.* Increasing in extent or severity; often used in reference to disease, such as civilization.

Prohibitionism, *n.* Teetotalitarianism.

Prohibitionist, *n.* An intemperate proponent of temperance. A superstitious person who thinks it possible to cast evil spirits out of a body politic by legislative incantation. A teetotalitarian.

Pro-Life, *adj.* Opposed to killing some people (or alleged people) under some circumstances.

Pro-Lifer, *n.* One who believes all human life is sacred—and who therefore is very happy that Josef Stalin was not aborted. One who wants the Chinese to conquer the world.

Promise, *v.* To give one's word. But if it is impossible to have one's cake and eat it too, then how is it possible to give one's word and keep it too?

Proofreader, *n.* One who looks over printers' proofs and overlooks errors in them.

Propaganda, *n.* Communication, such as this definition. Remember: What's proper for the goose is propaganda.

Property Tax, *n.* The rent paid to the supreme landlord, the government.

Prophet, *n.* One to whom Yahweh says, "Blah, blah, blah, blah, blah, blah, blah. Pass it on." One who speaks for a god too shy to speak for Himself. One of my favorite prophets is Dr. Joseph Jeffers, who has communicated directly with Yahweh, the Creator, who lives on the planet Orion. Here is part of the prophecy that Dr. Jeffers published in 1975:

> There will be a completely new political system in this country and other countries of the world. Yahweh, the Creator, is preparing the world for a one world government.
> After the Third World War, or Armageddon, everything that is evil or bad on the Earth will

be destroyed and only good and beautiful things will remain. It will be a world of peace, happiness and love among all mankind and Yahweh will set up his own king of kings, who will rule the whole Earth and the people will follow and obey the true Creator Yahweh .... Much of the destruction will take place in 1976 and this will be the year that will bring about the changes that were necessary in order for the world Utopia to be fulfilled. Beginning in June 1976—Armageddon, if not sooner. Destruction of the Berlin Wall will take place. Russia will occupy the Holy Land. Russia will make a deal to avoid war with China. Russia will attack the United States, secretly in 1975 and openly in 1976. Much trouble in Asia is coming. China and Russia will agree in occupying or controlling all Asia. Russian troops will invade some parts of Asia; Japan will cut the ribbon with the United States. New Zealand, Australia, America, Mexico, and Scandinavian countries will fall to the Communists. The Vatican will be controlled by the Communists. Fidel Castro will be out. Russia plans to attack the United States before our Bicentennial or before July 4, 1976. It will probably be on a Sunday like Pearl Harbor .... Ford will not finish his term. The facts will be known concerning President Ford's health and his wife's deteriorating health. Kissinger will be removed from his positions. Rockefeller will be the last President of the United States. He will declare martial law and bring about a complete dictatorship before Russia attacks .... The Messiah will speak to the world in 1976! Hold onto your hats- you haven't seen anything yet! Yes, in 1976, the Messiah will be seen on TV giving the last warning before the final destruction date! Keep a sharp lookout for this prophecy will surely come to pass in 1976!

Well, goshdarnit! I guess it all must have come to pass that one time that I blinked during 1976.

Prophet Muhammad, The, *n.* A figure whose likeness it is forbidden to depict. Must have been one ugly son of a bitch!

Prosperity, *n.* God's reward to the righteous—or to the wicked, as the case may be.

Prostitute, *n.* A venereal entrepreneur. One who fucks for bucks. One who does it for money. (See "Professional").

Protocols of the Learned Elders of Zion, n. A document that describes a plan to achieve world domination. Of course, as everybody knows, this document is a fraud, a fake, a forgery, a hoax, and in this case, what everybody knows is probably true. At any rate, I find it very interesting that the *Protocols*, which Henry Ford once said "fit in with what is going on," contain nothing whatsoever about Zionism and nothing about Jewish immigration to Palestine to set up a Jewish state there. Despite that, some conspiracy nuts have had the chutzpah to attribute the *Protocols* to the Zionists.

Proverb, *n.* A saying that condenses the wisdom of experience into a half-truth. Following are some lesser-known proverbs: (1) Nothing ventured, nothing lost. (2) Presents make the heart grow fonder. (3) People who live in glass houses shouldn't get stoned. (4) Two heads are better than none. (5) One man's meat is another man's sacred cow.

Providence, *n.* God supposedly sticking his nose into mundane matters, according to someone who has benefited from, or at least survived, said nose-sticking.

Psilocybe mexicana, *n.* A mushroom with a view.

Psychic Mafia, The, *n.* The Cosa Nostradamus, exposed by former medium M. Lamar Keene in his book bearing this title.

Psycho-Cybernetics, *n.* The magic power of self-delusion psychology, promulgated by Maxwell Schmaltz.

Psychokinesis, *n.* The power of sleight of hand over gray matter.

Psychopath, *n.* The path less traveled.

Psychosurgery, *n.* Healing the mind by destroying the brain.

Public, The, *n.* The most rapacious of the special interest groups.

Public Diplomacy, *n.* A propaganda euphemism for propaganda.

Public Opinion, *n.* The prevailing idiocies, delusions, and impossible dreams of the people collectively.

Public School, *n.* An institution where children receive government-approved indoctrination, as opposed to parent-approved indoctrination.

Publish or Perish, *phr.* Trick or treatise.

Puissant, *adj.* Not a pissant.

Punitive Damages, *n.* Damaging punishments.

Punk Funk, *n.* Hyped tripe.

Punk Rock, *n.* Proof that kids say the darndest things. A quasi-musical expression of adolescent rebelliousness.

Purge, *v.* To cleanse, commonly by means of a bloodbath.

Purism, *n.* Pure fanaticism.

Puritan, *n.* One who believes that even sex in the shower is filthy.

Purity of Arms, *n.* The Israeli term for the military practice of bending over backwards to avoid killing civilians. Unfortunately, when Israeli soldiers bend over backwards, it makes it more difficult for them to shoot straight and avoid killing civilians.

PUSH, *n.* The acronym for Jesse Jackson's organization People United to Shove Humanity.

Pythagoreanism, *n.* Math and myth.

Quagga, *n.* A South African equine with attributes of both the ass and the zebra that is now extinct, proving it was not fit to survive—so good riddance to the quagga!

Quaker, *n.* One who follows the Inner Light into outer darkness.

Quetzalcoatl, *n.* The feathered serpent. The Aztec god of transitional evolutionary forms.

Quotable, *adj.* Suitable for quotation, like, for example, the wonderfully witty definitions in *this* exceptionally excellent lexicon.

Rabbit's Foot, *n.* The left hind foot of a rabbit, carried as a good luck charm by those who ignore the bad luck of the rabbit it came from.

Racist, *n.* One who calls a spade a spade; one who tells it like it is, baby!

Rack, *n.* A machine for stretching the truth.

Radical Chic, *n.* Supporting the cause primarily for the effect.

Radical Traditionalist, *n.* A hunter-gatherer who spends his spare time writing books denouncing Judaism, the Hermetic conspiracy, and civilization.

Randi, James, *n.* A man who thinks the only thing dowsing rods are good for is spanking dowsers.

Randian, *n.* A Galt-ridden individual.

Randroid, *n.* A robotic Objectivist. Man *qua* tape recorder.

Rape, *n.* In Objectivism, the way in which a man of reason, purpose, and self-esteem expresses love at first sight.

Rapist, *n.* One who cannot get to first base and so steals home.

Rapture, *n.* The unbounded joy that will be experienced by those of us left behind after every fundamentalist Christian disappears from the face of the Earth (with a collective cry of "Beam me up, Goddy!".) An expression that is not in the Bible. "The Bible" is another expression that is not in the Bible.

Rapture of the Deep, *n.* The intoxication experienced by deep-sea divers from breathing compressed air. Not to be confused with Rapture of the Dip, the assumption into Heaven that a premil dip (premillenial dipsensationalist) mistakenly expects to experience any second now.

Rapture-Ready, *adj.* Not ready for no Rapture.

Rational Anti-Semitism, *n.* Hysterical Hitlerian heebie-jeebies.

Rationalist, *n.* One who puts Descartes before the horse sense. One who is blinded by the Enlightenment.

Reactionary, *n.* One who does not go with the

flow of progressive bullshit. One who longs for the good old days of the '50s—the 950s.

Reagan, Ronald, *n.* A white man in a white hat on a white horse in the White House. The Sheriff of the Free World. The Fastest Gun in the West. The great American president who saved us from the menace of Grenada.

Reagan Country, *n.* The valley of the shadow of death.

Reaganomics, *n.* Ronald Reagan's radical economics, involving cutting federal taxes and expenditures and increasing federal taxes and expenditures.

Reagan Revolution, *n.* A change in the course of the American ship of state by at least one or two degrees, I'm sure. As Gore Vidal has said, Reagan wants to get the government off our backs and onto our fronts.

Real American, *n.* One who does not wear a diaper on his head, though perhaps he should, considering what a shithead he is.

Realist, *n.* One who says reality is Silly Putty, then bounces it around for fun.

Reality, *n.* An escape from drugs.

Real Peace, *n.* The kind of peace that can only be achieved by real war.

Reason, *n.* The faculty with which one can find a reason for anything. The faculty that identifies and integrates the evidence provided by man's senses—and by books, newspapers, magazines, television, movies, the Internet, rumors, gossip, memories, imagination, dreams, hallucinations, and a vast array of illusory stimuli. Come on, Objectivists, do you really mean to pretend that Ayn Rand's ideas were derived purely from the evidence of her senses? Did Rand have any direct sensory evidence to account for, say, the Renaissance? Of course not. She wasn't there. But that didn't prevent her from pontificating dogmatically and ignorantly about it. (For an example of one aspect of the Renaissance about which Ayn Rand was apparently clueless, look up "Renaissance Neoplatonism," and tell me if you trust the evidence of your senses.)

Recreational Drugs, *n. pl.* The type of drugs popular among people in recreational vehicles.

Redistribution of Wealth, *n.* Robbing Peter to pay Paul, something that every government does. No, redistribution of wealth was not invented by Barack Obama or FDR or Woodrow Wilson or even Karl Marx. For example, when the state of Georgia held the Gold Lottery of 1832, which awarded to winners 40-acre tracts of land that belonged to the Cherokee, that was redistribution of wealth.

Reefer Madness, *n.* The insanity invariably inspired by smoking the Devil's weed, marijuana. It leads to loud music, illicit sex, and homicide. Yes, smoking marijuana always leads to homicide, preferably of some narc.

Reichstag Fire, *n.* A false false-flag operation. A widely accepted conspiracy theory claims that, one way or another, the Nazis set fire to the Reichstag building in 1933 to provide a pretext for cracking down on communists and other political opponents. However, in his book, *The Reichstag Fire: Legend and Reality*, Fritz Tobias made a convincing case that Marinus van der Lubbe was the lone arsonist, just as van der Lubbe himself claimed.

Reincarnate, *v.* To become a born-again Hindu.

Reincarnation, *n.* The recycling of a soul to preserve the ectoplasmic balance. Reincarceration.

Reliable Sources, *n., pl.* Sources judged to be reliable by someone whose judgment might not be.

Religion, *n.* A cult with clout. The opiate of the asses.

Rendezvous with Destiny, *n.* A *tête-à-tête* with TNT.

Reparations, *n., pl.* To the victims go the spoils.

Reporter, *n.* One who covers some of the news and covers up the rest.

Reprisal, *n.* In Israeli military practice, taking ten eyes for an eye.

Republic, *n.* A government which derives its just powers from the sanction of the victimized.

Republican, *n.* An elephant with Alzheimer's.

Respect, *v.* Fear.

Respectable, *adj.* Beneath contempt.

Retaliate, *v.* To take an eye for an eye (or in the case of Israel, to take a hundred eyes for an eye).

Revelations, *n.* The Hallelujacinations of St. John the Insane.

Revenge, *n.* Getting even—or getting even more than even.

Reverence, *n.* In the words of Ambrose Bierce, "The spiritual attitude of a man to a god and a dog to a man."

Revisionist Historian, *n.* One who knows that everything you know is wrong. A historian who loves the truth but not as much as he hates the establishment. One who knows that there are two sides to every genocide. A historian who seeks to set the record straight—or parallel with his own line of thought, at any rate. A historian who loves the truth enough to lie for it. A contra-Versailles historian.

Revolution, *n.* A game of musical chairs, the object of which is to end up occupying the seat of government. A gun-American activity.

Revolutionary, *n.* One who is willing, even eager, to throw the dice and overthrow the government.

Righteous Gentile, *n.* A useful idiot. "It is possible that George W. Bush was the most righteous gentile of our time.

Righteousness, *n.* The moral aspect of mighteousness.

Right-to-Work Law, *n.* A no-right-to-work-in-a-closed-shop law.

Riot, *n.* A natural disaster necessitating federal relief.

Ripe, *adj.* 1. Ready for plucking. 2. Ready for fucking.

Ripperology, *n.* The study of the "Jack the Ripper" murders, not the study of the "Yorkshire Ripper" murders, much less the study of the deeds of the "Shropshire Slasher." At last count, there were 43,246 leading suspects in the "Jack the Ripper" case.

Ritual Murder, *n.* Abracadaver.

Ritz, *n.* 1. A hotel noted for its opulence. 2. The brand of cracker one naturally orders from room service when staying at such a hotel.

Rock and Roll, *n.* Fuck-and-suck music. The Devil's favorite form of music. Following are the names of some of the Devil's favorite rock-and-roll bands: Cyrano and the Bushwackers; The Jewel-Encrusted Cattle Prods; Black Fag; The Rubber Barons; The Distilled Essence of Pessimism; The Scumsucking Dogs; The Nun-Fuckers; The Zealous Yes-Men; The Screaming

Egos; The Stupid Teenagers; Fermented Beetle Juice; The Lavender Dipshits; The Amazing Amazonian Manslaughterers; The Blazing Bozos; The Inconspicuous Nonconformists; The Dissident Bureaucrats; The Humongous Hummingbirds; Yakima Jockstrap; The Insane Canary; The Bullshit Radicals; The Plastic Rebels; Section 8 ½; The Latter-Day Sinners; Exploding Mastodons; Spears for Queers; The Avant-Gauche; The Drooling Dogs; The Pedantics; The Proud Morons; Led Zipper; Ded Leper; Black Sabbatini; Art Annoys; The Pretentious Wimps; The Bullshit Artistes; The Bang Gang; The Lovesick Octopus; Spastic Colon; The Brazen Hussies; Cherries Jubilee; The State-of-the-Art Hallucinations; The Banzai Dog Band; The Tough-Talking Adolescents; Jean d'Arc and the Flaming Faggots; The Doomed; Impending Disaster; The Finger Blisters; The Velvet Underwear; The Conspicuous Turkeys; The Obvious Phonies; The Stinking Assholes; Idiot's Delight; The Insane Librarians; The Lunatic Liberals; The Raving Amnesiacs; The Gorky Park Pigeons; The Monkey-Blowers; Sweet-and-Sour Jesus; The Appallingly Repetitious Punks; The All-Day Suckers; Holy Guacamole; Female Candy; The Dead Doorknobs; The Revelling Grovellers; The Pimply-Faced Pipsqueaks; The Beloved Sleazeballs; The Trendy Twits; The Banana-Split Beavers; Dead Air; The Gorgeous Dog Turds; Sacred Cockroaches; Savage Tomales; The Blond Beast; Jello Biafra's Rotting Corpse; The Consciousness-Expanding Furballs; The Gutless Gentiles; The Chickenshit Libertarians;

The Obscene Puritans; The Big Lie; Serial Killers from Sirius; The Hopped-Up Utopians; The Stray Hawgs; The Weaping Weasels; The Dog Pound Boys; The Blurb; The Holy Goats; The Cash; Hoop the Mottle; Pink Freud; The Dugly Ucklings; The Towering Eyefulls; The Burning Britches; and The Scrumptious Cunts.

Rocker, *n.* One who rocks. For example, Rudolf Rocker.

Rogue State, *n.* A state that commits the offense of impersonating the policeman of the world.

Rollins, L.A., *n.* A lexicographer with a Chip Smith on his shoulder.

Romany, *n.* A nation of shoplifters.

Ron Paul Revolution, The, *n.* A revolution that is not a revolution, at least not so far.

Rosicrucian, *n.* Originally, a supposed member of a supposed secret society whose supposed lips supposedly were Hermetically sealed.

Royalty, *n.* A share paid to a writer of the proceeds from the sale of his or her work, so called because it invariably enables him or her to live like royalty, such as an Ellery Queen or a Stephen King.

Rule of Law, The, *n.* The law of rulers.

Rumor, *n.* A story passing from mouth to mouth. For example, the story I was once told by someone claiming to know someone who supposedly knew the protagonist, to wit, the story that Danny Kaye, recipient of the Jean Hersholt Humanitarianism Award, eats his own shit, for health reasons, and calls it his "scrap iron."

Rumsfeld, Donald, *n.* Formerly, a rock star who trashed not just hotel rooms but whole hotels—and even whole countries! He is, however, no longer a rock star, and his reputation now lies buried in the Tomb of the Unknown Unknowns.

Russell, Charles Taze, *n.* A man who went from haberdashery to balderdashery when he organized the group now known as Jehovah's False Witnesses.

Russia, *n.* A riddle wrapped in a mystery inside an enigma behind an Iron Curtain.

Sacred, *adj*. Profane but pretentious.

Sacred Cow, *n*. A bovine deemed divine. Food for freethought.

Sadism, *n*. Taking pleasure from giving pain.

Sadist, *n*. One who likes to beat around the bush.

Safer Sex, *n*. Sex with Morley Safer.

Saint Augustine, *n*. A 4th- and 5th-century intellectual who abandoned the ridiculous myths and superstitions of the Manichees in order to embrace the ridiculous myths and superstitions of the Christians.

Saint Francis of Assisi, *n*. Saint Francis, a sissy.

Salivation, *n.* A prerequisite for salvation.

Saloon, *n.* A salon for the working class.

Salute, *n.* To honor formally, as by holding the tip of one's thumb against the tip of one's nose while wiggling one's fingers back and forth.

Salvation, *n.* God's merciful act of saving you from Himself.

Same-Sex Marriage, *n.* Something new under the sun and, therefore, a refutation of Ecclesiastes. A prerequisite for same-sex divorce.

Sanity, *n.* The madness of the majority.

Satan, *n.* The son, not the father, of lies.

Satanism, *n.* Organized blasphemy for black sheep. The flipside of Christianity.

Satanist, *n.* One who thinks Hell is cool. Anyone so designated by a raving religious fanatic.

Savage, Michael, *n.* A silly savage who tells even bigger whoppers than other lying Zionist warmongers. For example, Savage goes beyond the usual lie that Mahmoud Ahmadinejad, the president of Iran, has threatened to wipe Israel off the map; according to Savage, Ahmadinejad has threatened to kill every Jew in the world.

Scalper, *n.* A barbarous barber who takes much too much off the top.

Scarcity, *n.* Scare City.

Scholarship, *n.* A ship of educated fools.

Scholastic, *n.* An Aristotalitarian. A medieval theologian who wondered how many angels could fit on the pinnacle of his head.

Scholera, *n.* An acute, infectious academic disease characterized primarily by serious intestinal-fortitude disorders.

School Spirit, *n.* Ardent loyalty to the school one is forced to attend.

Science, *n.* The superstition of the enlightened.

Scientific Socialism, *n.* Socialistic scientism; materialistic millenarianism; mystical Marxism; clairvoyant communism.

Scientism, *n.* Worship of Science. The religion of many pseudo-skeptics.

Scientist, *n.* Formerly, a seeker of objective truth. Presently, a whore for big business and/or the state.

Scientologist, *n.* One who professes a belief in freedom of religion but not in freedom of speech.

Secession, *n.* The Declaration of Independence of the Confederacy (also known as the Untied States of America).

Second Amendment, The, *n.* The Constitutional Amendment guaranteeing the right to the pursuit of trigger-happiness.

Second Coming, The, *n.* The long-awaited return appearance by Jesus Christ Superstar.

Second-Generation Survivor, *n.* A second-generation jiver.

Second Sight, *n.* The kind of sight made possible by the third eye.

Secret Doctrine, The, *n.* A doctrine that isn't secret anymore, thanks to Blabbermouth Blavatsky.

Secret Society, *n.* A society that uses secret signs, oaths, rites, or symbols, such as the Cult of the All-Hearing Ear, the Square Chair Groups, the Perry Masons, the Pinkicrucians, the Elders of Albion, or the Wise Guys of Zion. According to Naomi Weisstein, Virginia Blaisdell, and Jesse Lemisch in *The Godfathers: Freudians, Marxists, and the Scientfic and Political Protection Societies*,

> there actually exist, in psychology, two secret societies where fifty or so of the "really excellent" young scientists get together to make themselves better scientists (and lo, how the mountains then resound with choruses of Melancholy Baby).

Security, *n.* Freedom from freedom.

Seeker, *n.* One who seeks but, contrary to Jesus, does not necessarily find. *Why did the seeker stick his head up his ass? Because his guru told him that to find the truth, he must look inside himself.*

Self-Censorship, *n.* Tying one's own tongue. The type of censorship preferred by self-reliant Americans. In the words of Ursula K. LeGuin, the "Stalin in the Soul." By the same token, the Hitler in the heart, the McCarthy in the mind, the Hier in the head, or the Schechter (in Canada, the Shefman) in the self.

Self-Defense, *n.* The God-given right to kill anyone who you paranoically presume might possibly attack you someday. Fortunately, God gave this right only to Israelis and Americans, not to Ayrabs or Muzzlems.

Self-Employed, *adj.* Self-enslaved. Self-exploited.

Self-Esteem, *n.* The self-generated hot air used to fuel oneself.

Self-Government, *n.* Self-enslavement. Government by someone else who belongs to the same group.

Self-Image, *n.* A self-portrait painted in pigments of the imagination.

Self-Pity, *n.* The art of whining, "Why me?"

Self-Reliant, *adj.* Able to dress oneself, to cut one's own hair, to grow one's own food and drugs, to do one's own thing, to pull one's own strings, to pull the wool over one's own eyes, to prepare one's own index, to remove one's own appendix, to blow one's own nose, to blow one's own horn, to blow one's own skinflute, to blow one's own mind, to blow one's own brains out, and to read one's own eulogy.

Semen, *n.* The glue of love.

Senseless Murder, *n.* The kind of murder that makes no sense, as distinguished from a sensible murder, the only kind of murder that a sensible person, wearing sensible shoes, would commit.

Serf, *n.* A Euro-peon.

Serial Killer, *n.* A murder addict. According to conspiracy theorist Michael Hoffman II, the term "serial killer" is heard in the unconscious group mind of the masses as "cereal killer," suggesting human sacrifices to the pagan goddess Ceres. The following are some questions that I've addressed to Hoffman that he has not answered: Is "mass murderer" heard in the unconscious group mind of the masses as "Mass (i.e., Communion or the Eucharist) murderer," suggesting human sacrifices to Jesus Christ? Is "parish priest" heard in the unconscious group mind of the masses as "perish, priest," suggesting the telling of a priest to die? Is "lone assassin" heard in the unconscious group mind of the masses as "loan assassin," suggesting a killer working for the bankers? Is "missile attack" heard in the unconscious Group Mind of the masses as "missal [prayerbook] attack," suggesting a Christian religious war? Is "sleigh bells" heard in the unconscious group mind of the masses as "slay belles," suggesting an order to kill popular, attractive girls or women? Is "genocide" heard in the unconscious group mind of the masses as "Jennacide, " suggesting the killing of someone named "Jenna"? Is "deliverer" [i.e., savior] heard in the unconscious group mind of the masses as "de-liverer" [i.e., remover of one's liver], suggesting the liver-eating eagle Zeus used to punish Prometheus? Is "Dachau" heard in the unconscious group mind of the masses as "Doc, ow," suggesting painful medical atrocities? Etc., etc., etc.

Sermon on the Mount, *n.* The sermon in which Jesus, according to the Gospels, did not see eye to eye with Moses *vis-à-vis* an eye for an eye. An illustration of the immutable nature of "God's law"? Possibly not.

Servile, *adj.* Vile, sir.

Settle Down, *v.* To emulate sediment.

Sex, *n.* A pleasant combination of suction and friction. Fun with dickin' Jane. One of God's greatest gifts to the sinful.

Sexism, *n.* An egregious manifestation of man's inhumanity to his fellow man. A new heresy—or, rather, a new *his*esy.

Shaker, *n.* One who shakes, as distinguished from a Quaker (one who quakes) or a fakir (one who fakes).

Shaman, *n.* A contraction of "sham man." One particularly well-known shaman is Don Juan, Carlos Castaneda's fictional creation, as was demonstrated by Richard de Mille in *Castaneda's Journey: The Power and the Allegory*.

Shambhala, *n.* A fake bhala. Not to be confused

with Shangri-la, which is a fake Shambhala.

Shermer, Michael, *n.* A pseudo-skeptical schoolmarm.

Shiftless, *adj.* Working no shift, neither the day shift, the swing shift, the midnight shift, nor even the paradigm shift.

Short, Short, Short Story, *n.* An extremely short story, such as "In the beginning, there was nothing. There is still nothing. THE END."

Shylock, *n.* One who wants the pound of flesh—or the flesh of Pound.

Silent Night, *n.* A Christmas Eve when no one disturbs their neighbors by singing annoying Christmas carols.

Sin, *n.* A synonym for "fun." A god first worshipped in ancient Harran but now universally revered.

Single-Taxer, *n.* One who advocates one tax too many.

Singular, *adj.* As unusual as the incident chronicled in *Konungs skuggsjá* (c. 956 AD):

> There happened in the borough of Cloera, one
> Sunday while the people were at Mass, a marvel.
> In this town there is a church to the memory
> of St. Kinarus. It befell that a metal anchor was
> dropped from the sky, with a rope attached to
> it, and one of the sharp flukes caught in the
> wooden arch above the church door. The people
> rushed out of the church and saw in the sky
> a ship with men on board, floating at the end

of the anchor cable, and they saw a man leap overboard and pull himself down the cable to the anchor as if to unhook it. He appeared as if he were swimming in water. The folk rushed up and tried to seize him; but the bishop forbade the people to hold the man for fear it might kill him. The man was freed and hurried up the cable to the ship where the crew cut the rope and the ship rose and sailed away out of sight. But the anchor is in the church as a testimony to this singular occurrence.

Sinner, *n.* A cosmic criminal.

Are you a sinner? Of course you are. So consider the words of the Reverend Jonathan Edwards:

The God that holds you over the pit of hell, much as one holds a spider, or some loathsome insect, over the fire, abhors you and is dreadfully provoked; his wrath towards you burns like fire; he looks upon you as worthy of nothing else but to be cast into the fire; he is of purer eye than to bear to have you in his sight; you are ten thousand times as abominable in his eyes, as the most hateful and venomous serpent is in ours. You have offended him infinitely more than ever a stubborn rebel did his prince; and yet it is nothing but his hand that holds you from falling into the fire every moment; it is ascribed to nothing else that you did not go to hell last night; that you were suffered to wake again in this world, after you closed your eyes to sleep; and there is no other reason to be given why you have not dropped into hell since you arose in the morning, but that God's hand has held you up: there is no other reason to be given why you have not gone to hell, since you have set here in the house of God, provoking his pure eyes by your sinful wicked manner of attending his solemn worship: yea, there is nothing else that is to be given as a reason why you do not this very moment drop down into hell. O sinner! consider the fearful danger you are in: it is a great furnace of wrath, a wide and bottomless pit, full of the fire of wrath, that you are held over in the hand of God, whose wrath is provoked and incensed as much against you, as against many of the damned in hell: you hang by a slender thread, with the flames of divine wrath flashing about it, and ready every moment to singe it and burn it asunder; and you have no interest in any Mediator, and nothing to lay hold of to save yourself, nothing to keep off the flames of wrath, nothing of your own, nothing that you have ever done, nothing that you can do, to induce God to spare you one moment .... It is everlasting wrath. It would be dreadful to suffer this fierceness and wrath of Almighty God one moment; but you must suffer it to all eternity: there will be no end to this exquisite, horrible misery: when you look forward you will see a long forever, a boundless duration before you, which will swallow up your thoughts and amaze your soul; and you will absolutely despair of ever having any deliverance, any end, any mitigation, any rest at all; you will know certainly that you must wear out long ages, millions and millions of ages, in wrestling and conflicting with the Almighty's merciless vengeance; and then, when you have so done, when so many ages have actually been spent by you in this manner, you will know your punishment will indeed be infinite. Oh, who can express what the state of a soul in such circumstances is! All that we can possibly say about it gives but a very feeble, faint representation of it; it is inexpressible and inconceivable; for who knows the power of God's anger?

Sirius, _n._ The hidden supreme god of the secret societies of the West, just like Jahbulon, Lucifer, Satan, etc.

Sitchinite, _n._ A disciple of Zecharia Sitchin,

who believes that ancient people lacked imagination—unlike modern people, such as Zecharia Sitchin.

Situationist, *n.* One who subverts the society of the spectacle by making a spectacle of himself. One who is skeptical of the spectacle. One who is boring from within. (Vaneigem if they can't take a joke.)

Skeptic, *n.* One who doubts what he does not want to believe and believes what he does not want to doubt.

Skepticism, *n.* A no-bull attitude.

Skinhead, *n.* One who shaves his head and is either a racist or anti-racist bigot.

Skoptsy, *n.* A member of a possibly defunct Russian sect who was man enough to emasculate himself for the Kingdom of Heaven's sake, as per Matthew 19:12.

Slime Mold, *n.* The third cousin several times removed of Richard Dawkins.

SMI²LE, *n.* The optimystic science-fiction religion of Timothy Leary. I am sometimes leery of Leary because sometimes, I have no idea what out-of-this world he's talking about.

Smoker, *n.* An ambulatory air-polluter.

Smuggler, *n.* A contrabandito.

So-Called Rich, The, *n.* The rich, as referred to by Rich Limbau—er...I mean, Rush Limbaugh.

Socialism, *n.* An indigestible omelet.

Socialist Realism, *n.* Socialist Romanticism. The attempt to draw a pretty picture of the Soviet system. Chesterton said that art "consists in drawing the line somewhere." In the Soviet Union, the line is drawn by the Communist Party.

Social Security, *n.* Subsidized senility.

Socrates, *n.* Plato's sockpuppet.

Soft Rock, *n.* A contradiction in terms.

Soldier, *n.* One who pretends to be a defender of freedom; in reality, a hired gun for a government that violates freedom.

Solidarity, *n.* The feeling of brotherhood felt by American capitalists for Polish workers.

Solipsist, *n.* One who has only himself to blame. One for whom masturbation is the only kind of sex possible. One whose only option is to bowl alone.

Somoza Family, *n.* Formerly, the Nicaraguafellers.

Soon, *adv.*, Sometime within the next trillion years or so. (This is the meaning of the word as it is used in certain prophetic writings, such as The Holy Qur'an.)

Soothsayer, *n.* One who says "sooth."

Soul, *n.* An invisible, intangible, inaudible, tasteless, and odorless—but marketable—entity.

Sound Doctrine, *n.* Doctrine that is sound. More fully, doctrine that is sound and fury, signifying nothing.

Sour Grapes, *n., pl.* Fruits that, when fermented, produce fine whines.

Southern Baptist, *n.* A Baptist who is even stupider than other Baptists.

Southern Belle, *n.* A Dixieland dingaling.

Soviet Dissident, *n.* A Zionist conformist.

Soviet Imperialism, *n.* The last, best hope of American imperialism.

Soviet Russia, *n.* Formerly, the future—but it didn't work.

Specter, Arlen, *n.* A specter who is haunting America.

Speleotherapy, *n.* Medical treatment utilizing the curative properties of the microclimate of underground caves. The indispensable word was coined by Soviet physicians to identify a regimen including plenty of exercise working in salt mines, which they frequently prescribed for those sick of the Soviet regime. Because salt mines have no allergens but are rich in minute salt particles, speleotherapy is considered especially beneficial for treating bronchial complaints, but it can be used to treat virtually any type of complaint.

Spelling, *n.* The act of one who spells words, such as one who spells "TV" as "T & A."

Spice, *n.* The plural of "spouse."

Spitballs, *n., pl.* Weapon systems that are very low-tech, very inexpensive, and, therefore, of no interest to war profiteers, even though they are perfectly adequate for protecting the country against imaginary menaces.

Spontaneous Combustion, *n.* Making an ash of oneself.

Square Dance, *n.* Obviously, a dance for squares.

Stalinism, *n.* Rugged collectivism. Dog-eat-dog socialism.

Standing Army, *n.* A menace, according to Thomas Jefferson and other Founding Fathers. I agree, but I will add that, in my opinion, a standing army is not as much of a menace as a marching army.

Stand-Up Comedian, *n.* A humorist on his hind legs.

Stars and Stripes, The, *n.* The Blood-Spattered Banner; Old Gory; That Grand Old Rag.

Statecraft, *n.* Assoulcraft. The Triumph of George Will.

State of Nature, *n.* A justification for the nature of the state.

Statutory Rape, *n.* Violation by a statute.

Steel, *n.* One of two metals from which guitars are made, the other being lead. Of course, lead guitars are much more common than steel guitars.

Stereotype, *n.* A standardized image imposed upon all the diverse individuals comprising some group. For example, in contemporary American culture, Nazis are stereotyped as sadistic mass murderers, anti-Semites are stereotyped as Nazis, and Holocaust revisionists are stereotyped as anti-Semites. Interestingly enough, it is precisely the same people who most vigorously preach against stereotyping who most rigorously practice the stereotyping of Nazis, anti-Semites, and Holocaust revisionists. As a result, Rabbi Marvin Hier can tell the press that "Every time you give these Holocaust revisionists a microphone, they kill the victims of Hitler's Final Solution a second time," and none of our avatars of tolerance even bats an eyelash at this incitement to kill Holocaust revisionists; after all, if Holocaust revisionists are mass murderers, as the rabbi says, then killing Holocaust revisionists is an act of justice, isn't it? I can hardly wait for the day when Rabbi Hier rules the world and his "Museums of Tolerance" dot the planet, each of them containing a gas chamber for the execution of those "paper Eichmanns," the Holocaust revisionists. What a wonderful world it will be! Heil Hier!

Stigmata, *n., pl.* Bloody miracles, showing that Yahweh has the aesthetic sensibility of a teenage horror fan. Come on, Yahweh, knock it off! If You're going to reveal Your presence through miracles, stop going for the gross-out and try something beautiful for a change. Show some class, Yahweh!

Stirnerite, *n.* Just another unique one like everyone else. One who worships the I-con. Someone who may have missed Stirner's point.

Straight Shooter, *n.* One who, like George W. Bush, is forthright and honest, according to those who are not.

Strategic Defense Initiative, *n.* Raygunomics.

String Theorist, *n.* One who believes that itsy-bitsy, teeny-weeny little stringy thingies are the fundamental doohickies of the universe.

Strong on Defense, *phr.* Willing, even eager, to spend money on the military like a drunken sailor with only one weekend left to live.

Subsidy, *n.* Government aid to a private commercial enterprise deemed beneficial to the public—but not by the public. Government aid to the plunderprivileged.

Success, *n.* The bitch-goddess that failed.

Succulent, *adj.* Worthy of being sucked. This word is analogous to "fucculent," meaning worthy of being fucked.

Suffer, *v.* According to Buddha, to be human. According to Judah, to be a Jew.

Suffrage, *n.* The right to choose the horn of a dilemma by which one shall be gored.

Suicide, *n.* Taking one's life—too seriously.

Summer, *n.* Simmer.

Summit, *n.* The height of diplomatic futility.

Sun, *n.* The face of God. But where, oh where, is His bod? A great big lightbulb up above the Earth. As pointed out by Wilbur Glenn Voliva,

> The idea of a sun millions of miles in diameter and 91,000,000 miles away is silly. The sun is only 32 miles across and not more than 3,000 miles from the Earth. It stands to reason it must be so. God made the sun to light the Earth, and therefore must have placed it close to the task it was designed to do.

Superstition, *n.* Another person's religion.

Supplicant, *n.* An independent person who is willing and able to stand on his own two knees.

Surgical Strike, *n.* An accidental bombing of a hospital's operating room.

Surrealism, *n.* An advertisement for utopia and a utopia for advertisers. Symbolshevism.

Suspect, *n.* One who is under suspicion of behaving like those who are above it.

Sustenance, *n.* Means of living, such as bread. But remember, man does not live by bread alone but by circuses as well.

Sycophant, *n.* One who seeks upward mobility

through upward sucking.

Synchronicity, *n.* The city of meaningful coincidences where, for example, while reading a book about nanotechnology, one hears the radio play an oldie titled "Neenie Nana Nana Nunu."

Syphilis, *n.* One of the many ills that, according to sexist Greek mythology, originally came from Pandora's box.

Szasz, *n., pl.* Tools for cutting us loose from the straightjacket of psychiatric ideology.

Tautology, *n.* A statement as empty as the head from which it issues, such as the following revelation from Ronald Reagan: "It's the unnecessary regulations that we don't need."

Tax, *n.* A payment made to the government for servitude rendered.

Tax, *v.* To fleece the sheep; to pluck the geese; to milk the cowed.

Tax Dodger, *n.* A term of opprobrium for one who keeps his own money. One who never gives a bloodsucker an even break.

Taxpayer, *n.* One who renders unto a seizer what is not the seizer's. One who feeds the mouth that puts the bite on him. An April fool.

Technology, *n.* Practical magic.

Technophile, *n.* A technofool. One who prefers Frankenfrankfurter. One who looks forward to owning the first nuclear-powered nose-hair trimmer.

Telepathy, *n.* A means of communication cheaper to use than a telephone but possibly not quite as reliable.

Televangelist, *n.* A bible- and bimbo-banger.

Television, *n.* An electronic Cyclops.

Tender, *adj.* Readily yielding to blade or teeth: said of food, such as the tender hearts of Christian missionaries or the tender feet of the Donner Party.

Terrorism, *n.* The nemesis of tourism. Intentional attacks on innocent civilians, such as those innocent civilians in the US Marine barracks in Beirut, Lebanon, in 1983. Intentional attacks on innocent oil pipelines.

Terrorist, *n.* An aspiring statesman. One who believes that dynamite makes right.

Tetragrammaton, *n.* A polysyllabic name for a four-letter word, YHWH.

Thanksgiving Day, *n.* A day when Americans give thanks that they are not turkeys, even though many of them actually are.

Theist, *n.* One who plays "heads I win, tails you lose" with atheists. Thus, for a theist, the apparent existence of regularities in nature constitute proof of the existence of a Creator; meanwhile, the existence of *irregularities* in nature (e.g., miracles) also proves the existence of a Creator. So you see, kiddies, for a theist who's already got his feeble mind made up, *everything* is proof of the existence of God!

Theocracy, *n.* Rule by God, *i.e.*, anarchy. Rule by people pretending to represent God. The integration of church and state, mosque and state, or synagogue and state. A holy alliance of brute faith and blind force.

Theodicy, *n.* The making of weak excuses for an omnipotent god. Theoidiocy.

Theology, *n.* The -ology of -ologies. During the Middle Ages, the iron maiden of philosophy.

Thief, *n.* A member of the species *Homo rapiens*, the man who seizes. One who has been blessed with the gift of grab, a gift that keeps on giving. The distinguishing characteristic of a thief is the opposable thumb, which enables him to seize the property of others.

Thin Air, *n.* A valuable natural resource out of which money can be created.

Thinking, *n.* A satanic activity and a leading cause of civilization. An un-American activity. Walter Freeman, a professor of neuropathology and practitioner of psychosurgery, is reported to have said, "Society can accommodate itself to the most humble laborer, but justifiably distrusts the mad thinker.... Lobotomized patients make rather good citizens."

Remember, if God had wanted us to think, He would have given us brains.

Third World, The, *n.* The Third-Rate World.

Thought Experiment, *n.* Not an experiment.

Thule Society, *n.* The Illuminazis.

Time, *n.* Our mortal enemy. We've got to kill time before time kills us.

Timorous, *adj.* As courageous as the American mass media, as, for example, in their coverage of the US government–approved Indonesian invasion of East Timor.

Tithe, *n.* To give ten percent of one's income to Jerry Falwell, who then gives ten percent of that to God.

Tobacco, *n.* A plant whose leaves are most pleasure-giving not when smoked or snuffed but when eschewed.

Tomboy, *n.* A girl engaged in sex-role subversion. A woman similarly engaged is a "thomasman."

Tongue Twister, *n.* A word or phrase difficult to articulate quickly, for example, "How much wood would George Woodcock cock if George Woodcock would cock wood?"

Torture, *n.* Ways of making people talk—after they've stopped screaming. The infliction of pain and terror on a prisoner to extract information—or just for the fun of it. Methods of interrogation that the US government absolutely must be able to use, according to many Republicans and other sadists.

Total Depravity, *n.* In Calvinism, the tendency of human nature to turn away from Calvinism.

Tough Times, *n. pl.* Times when the folks who work on Wall Street can no longer afford a $600 bottle of wine with their meals and have to settle for a $60 bottle.

Traditionalist, *n.* A slave of the dead.

Transcendental Wisdom, *n.* Wisdom that transcends the wisdom of the wisdom teeth.

Transgressive, *adj.* Naughty and therefore nice, according to a politically correct academic.

Translator, *n.* A Catullus-mutilator.

Transportation, *n.* The business of conveying from one pocket to another.

Transubstantiation, *n.* A supperstition.

Trappist, *n.* A monk who has vowed to keep his trap shut. If only all clergy would do likewise.

Trilateral Commission, *n.* According to David Rockefeller, "a group of concerned citizens interested in fostering greater understanding and cooperation among international allies." According to Antony Sutton, an infernal triangle. According to me, the Trilateral Commission is just a bunch of scum- and moneybags.

Trinitarian, *n.* One who believes that one plus one plus one equals one.

Trinity, *n.* Three gods for the price of one—but still no bargain.

Trophy Wife, *n.* A mantelpiece.

Trotskyist, *n.* One who believes Napoleon Trotsky wouldn't have killed quite as many people as Snowball Joe Stalin.

Truman, Harry S., *n.* The a-hole who dropped the A-bomb. A critical-mass murderer. The US president who gave 'em hell in Hiroshima and Nagasaki.

In his foreword to Israel Shahak's book *Jewish History, Jewish Religion*, Gore Vidal wrote,

> Sometime in the late 1950s, that world-class gossip and occasional historian, John F. Kennedy, told me how, in 1948, Harry S. Truman had been pretty much abandoned by everyone when he came to run for president. Then an American Zionist brought him two million dollars in cash, in a suitcase, aboard his whistlestop campaign train. "That's why our recognition of Israel was rushed through so fast."

I wonder if there is any connection between this story and the better-known one about the sign on Truman's desk in his White House office that read, "The buck stops here!"

Truth, *n.* Apparently, a very good thing since

every liar and every raving, dogmatic fanatic loves it above all else.

Truthseeker, *n.* Truthsucker. One who seeks what he does not tell.

TV, *n.* Transcendental vegetation, America's most popular method of meditation.

TV Evangelist, *n.* A holy high-roller, such as Jerry Foolwell, Jimmy Swaggering Braggart, or Jack Van Wimpe.

TV Star, *n.* A mediacrity.

Twilight Zone, *n.* The fifth dimension, where Rod Serling suffers the punishment of having to watch perpetual reruns of *Night Gallery*.

Twinfucker, *n.* A doppelganger-banger.

Two-Party System, *n.* A political system that, in theory, gives voters 200% as much choice as a one-party system—and 20% as much choice as a ten-party system. A political system that is more fun than a one-party system but not as much fun as a three-party or four-party or five-party system.

Ugly American, *n.* An American who looks in the mirror and sees the fairest of them all.

Ulysses, *n.* A novel by James Joyce. Sylvia-Beach literature.

Unanimity, *n.* Completely concealed disagreement.

Unbeliever, *n.* One who might believe all sorts of things but just not the same exact things that you believe.

Underground Economy, *n.* The secret sector.

Underground Press, *n.* All the news that misfits print.

Unfair Competition, *n.* Successful competition.

Unification Church, *n.* The marriage of the Sun and the Moon.

Unilateral Disarmament, *n.* Any miniscule reduction in US military spending.

Unimpeachable, *adj.* Not holding public office.

Union of Egoists, The, *n.* A union with little bargaining power and no pension.

Unitarian Universalism, *n.* The religion for people who think they are thinking people.

United States Government, The, *n.* A Ben Franklinstein monster.

Unity, *n.* A state of general discord and mutual bullshitting.

University, *n.* The antithesis of diversity.

Unperson, *n.* In Orwell's *1984*, a person who does not exist and who never existed. As O'Brien told Winston Smith,

> Posterity will never hear of you. You will be lifted clean out from the stream of history. We shall turn you into gas and pour you into the stratosphere. Nothing will remain of you: not a name in a register, not a memory in a living brain. You will be annihilated in the past as well as in the future. You will never have existed.

In an afterword to *1984*, Erich Fromm wrote,

> Books like Orwell's are powerful warnings, and it would be most unfortunate if the reader smugly interpreted *1984* as another description of Stalinist barbarism, and if he does not see that it means us, too.

Indeed. In "Requiem For A Writer," his introduction to *The Rabelaisian Letters of Jack Woodford* (1977), Jess E. Stewart wrote,

> Orwell's *1984* .... depicts how enemies of the state disappear without a trace, as though they had never been born, as though their work never existed. Take *The Writer's Handbook* edited by A.S. Burack for the year 1947. There is a chapter by Anne Hamilton where she mentions Jack Woodford's *Writing and Selling* (a revision of *Trial and Error*) on page 127. Nine years later *The Writer's Handbook* was reissued. Anne Hamilton's chapter is still presented in the new edition. However, mention of Jack Woodford in the same paragraph heading, "The Important Synopsis" is neatly lifted out and replaced by a stiff sentence which appears as though it were an insertion by an editor: "... making an outline ... common procedure ... etc."

Unrequited Love, *n.* Love that is paid back with disinterest.

Upbringing, *n.* A bringdown.

Uplifting, *adj.* Lifting up; raising aloft; elevating: said, for instance, about photos of naked women.

USS Liberty, , *n.* The US Navy's intelligence ship that Israeli forces attacked during the Six-Day War of 1967, wounding more than 100, killing more than 30 American crewmen, and providing one more of the many reasons why Israel is so widely regarded as the US' best and most reliable ally in the Middle East.

Utilitarian, *n.* A pig in shit.

Utility, *n.* A measure of well-being that defies

measurement.

Utopia, *n.* The best of all impossible worlds. A product of myopia.

Utopian, *n.* One whose consciousness has been raised all the way to Cloudcuckooland.

Utopianism, *n.* A nowheresy.

Vain, *n*. A foreign domain in which many a soldier has died.

Veal, *n*. Meat that is not merely murder but child murder.

Veterans of Foreign Wars, *n*. Veterans of imperialist wars.

Vietnam, *n*. Former name of the nation now known as "Sovietnam."

Village, *n*. What it takes to raise a village idiot.

Virgin, *n*. A carnal ignoramus.

Virgin Mary, The, *n*. Mary, who had a little Lamb.

Voluntary, *adj*. Proceeding from one's own free choice, under threat of compulsion.

Vonu, _n._ Invulnerability to coercion, a condition fully attainable only by the dead.

Voyeurism, _n._ Peek experience.

Walmart, *n.* A company that directly provides many low-paying jobs in the US and indirectly provides many even-lower-paying jobs in China.

Walnut, *n.* A type of nut that, as far as I know, is not a health nut, a gun nut, a conspiracy nut, or a religious nut.

Wannsee Protocol, The, *n.* The Protocol of the Learned Elders of Zyklon.

War, *n.* The racket that makes a racket. The answer to a war profiteer's prayer. Apparently, a very bad thing since every warmonger abhors it. A means of torture that is not opposed by warmongers such as John McCain.

War Criminal, *n.* Anyone so designated by the infallible Simon Wiesenthal, Nazifinder General, or any other Nazi-hunter. One who does not abide by the rules for properly conducting mass slaughter.

War on Drugs, *n.* A war to make the world safe for alcoholism.

War on Poverty, *n.* One of Lyndon Johnson's no-win wars.

War Profiteering, *n.* Parasitism in the name of patriotism. *The Profiteer Hymn*:

> *From the hauls of Halliburton*
> *To the Carlyle Group's gravy,*
> *We have seized our country's money*
> *From the National Treasury.*
> *First to hype a phony menace*
> *And to foment baseless fears,*
> *We are proud to bear the title*
> *Of venal war profiteers.*

Waterboarding, *n.* An extreme sport in which many Muslims have participated in recent years.

Watergate, *n.* Nixon's Waterloo. A third-rate crime of the century.

Weapons of Mass Destruction, *n., pl.* The most dangerous weapons in the world, so dangerous that they constitute an intolerable threat, even when they do not exist.

Webster, *n.* A weaver, such as, for example, Nesta Webster, who weaved Byzantine tales of Bavarian Illuminati intrigue into a tangled web.

Welfare Statist, *n.* One who seeks to promote

the general welfare by making welfare general.

Weltschmerz, *n.* Germanic depression.

Wetback, *n.* A participant in the Mexodus for whom the water did not part.

We the People, *n. pl.* What do you mean "We," white man?

Wheel in the Head, *n.* A mobile metaphor for a fixed idea.

Whiskey, *n.* The spirit of '94.

White Lie, *n.* A lie intended to spare someone's feelings—one's own.

White Supremacist, *n.* An inferior white man. Anyone so designated by a rainbow supremacist.

Whitman, Charles, *n.* A practical surrealist.

Wiesel, Elie, *n.* The sacred weasel of the Holocaust cult. Wiesel speaks in the name of memory, which undoubtedly is why he has asserted the following historical falsehoods: (1) There were never any religious persecutions instigated, organized, or implemented by Jews; (2) Jews have never hated their enemies; and (3) Jews have never become executioners when they have had power and their enemies none. Wiesel has characterized the works of Holocaust revisionists as "the recent attempts to kill the victims again." Wiesel himself must be a resurrected victim of the homicidal steam chambers of Treblinka—he's so full of hot air!

Wiggle, *n.* The *real* women's movement.

Windfall Profits Tax, *n.* Windfall tax profits.

Windowpane Acid, *n.* A detergent for cleaning the doors of perception.

Witch, *n.* An unidentified flying sex object.

Witch-Burning, *n.* The most appropriate way to send an evil woman to Hell. Although the practice was once common, its extent has sometimes been exaggerated. According to Ashley Montagu and Edward Darling, the movie *I Married a Witch* opened with a scene of witch-burning in 17th-century New England; but, in fact, England and the English colonies in America did not burn witches—they hanged them. During the well-known Salem witch-hunt, thirteen witches were hanged, while, for a change of pace, one witch was pressed to death. According to Montague Summers,

> The terrible Baltyvaden tragedy which was heard at Clonmel [Ireland] in 1895, and which is continually referred to as a "witch-burning," is wholly misnamed. The poor woman who was placed upon the kitchen fire by her own family and burned so that she died was not tortured because she was a witch, but in the belief that the real wife had been taken away and a fairy changeling substituted in her place; when the latter was subjected to the ordeal of fire it would vanish, and the wife would be restored.

Word, *n.* A weapon in the war of ideas. But remember, propagandists—He who lives by the word shall die by the word.

Work, *n.* A four-letter word, the most offensive obscenity of them all. I confess that I do not want to work at all and that my ambition is to be a full-time playboy. For a fascinating account of the origin and development of my anti-work ethic, see my forthcoming work, *It Usually Begins With Maynard G. Krebs.*

Work Ethic, *n.* Slave morality.

World Federalism, *n.* Government über alles.

World War I, *n.* The Great War. Even better than the sequel, which was only The Good War.

World War II, *n.* The bigger-budget, bigger-cast sequel to World War I that was also more successful at the box office. The six-year period from 1939 to 1945, during which, 60 million people died for Danzig. The Good War, but, to borrow a line from Ayn Rand, good for whom and by what standard? The Triumph of the Won't. The triumph of good over evil, according to pseudoskeptic Michael Shermer and other believers in the comic-book version of the war.

Worship, *n.* In the words of Ambrose Bierce, "Homo Creator's testimony to the sound construction and fine finish of Deus Creatus."

Wrong, *adj.* In agreement with fifty million Frenchmen.

Xmas, *n.* A day celebrating the birth of Our Lord and Savior, Malcolm X.

X-Ray Vision, *n.* A superpower useful to a crime-fighter—or a voyeur.

Yahweh, *n.* Not my way.

Yank, *n.* Jerk.

Yankee, *n.* One who is yanked, as distinguished from a "yanker," who does the yanking.

Yarmulka, *n.* A B'nai B'rith b'eanie.

Yellow Rain, *n.* A mixture of beeshit and bullshit. Not to be confused with a "golden shower," which is simply piss.

Yellow Ribbon, *n.* A self-awarded decoration for cowardice.

Zebra, *n.* A bra 25 sizes larger than an A-bra.

Zeitgeist, *n.* The dominant spook of the time.

Zen Master, *n.* A drill sergeant of the spirit. One who knows the sound of one hand slapping (the face of an aspirant).

Zenophobia, *n.* An irrational fear and hatred of paradoxes.

Zionism, *n.* Out of the ghettoes and into the Ghetto State. A movement for Jewish settlement in Palestine to make the desert Bloom's. The problem of which it purports to be the solution.

Zionist, *n.* An Israel estate agent. One who abominates, and emulates, the Nazis. A paranoid parasite. A bigot who wants the Jews to go back where they came from.

Zionist Propaganda, *n.* AIPAC of lies. Hebrew National baloney. Kristol blue(-and-white) persuasion. A commonly used synonym for "Zionist propaganda" is "the news."

From his book *Crossroads to Israel 1917–1948*, here is Christopher Sykes discussing the arrival at Haifa of Exodus 1947, a ship carrying 4,500 Jewish refugees:

> The Zionists had developed what may be called a boat-propaganda technique which was skillful but often erred on the side of excessive zeal. In his book Major R.D. Wilson, referring to a previous boat incident, tells at first hand of "the exhibition on one occasion of a one-year-old child who died at sea some days previously, with the statement to the press: 'The dirty Nazi-British assassins suffocated this innocent victim with gas.'" (Major Wilson goes on: "The *sotto voce* remark, 'It's not against you, it's for the Press,' made by one of the more moderate passengers to some of the troops hardly compensated.")

Zog, *n.* Formerly, the king of Albania. Not to be confused with ZOG, the current king of America.

Zombie, *n.* A fashionable—but not necessarily fashion-conscious—monster.

Zygote, *n.* A human being, just like you and me. Hath not a zygote eyes? Hath not a zygote hands, organs, dimensions, senses, affections, passions? If you prick them, do they not bleed? If you tickle them, do they not laugh? And if you wrong them, shall they not revenge?

Also available from

THE PORTABLE L.A. ROLLINS

The Myth of Natural Rights

Revised & Expanded

In *Lucifer's Lexicon*, Rollins defines "natural rights" as "walls made of wind." They won't stop bullets. They won't keep people from ripping off your property. They won't even stop the govern- ment from putting you in a concentration camp or executing you. About the only thing a "natural right" will stop is enlightened thinking on the ethics of liberty. Once you've read *The Myth of Natural Rights*, you'll be able to put those imaginary protectors of freedom back in the museums where they belong.

In one compact work, L.A. Rollins shatters the myth of natural rights while exposing the "bleed- ing-heart libertarians" that promote it. With careful research and ample documentation, he shows that thinkers like Ayn Rand, Murray Rothbard, Tibor Machan, and Samuel Konkin not only violate reason and logic in their defense of natural rights but also violate the standards they set for themselves.

Back in print for the first time in years, this new- ly revised edition features an insightful introduction by the Stirnerite-libertarian blogger TGGP, a new afterword by the author, and extensive commentary from the controversy that surrounded the books ini- tial release.

CPSIA information can be obtained
at www.ICGtesting.com
Printed in the USA
BVHW032340060822
643973BV00010B/1006